Praise for *Conversations Worth Having*

"Groundbreaking! Jackie and Cheri provide a great approach to improving communication in any setting. To be a great leader, read this book!"
—**Loyd Beal III, Lieutenant Colonel, US Army**

"This is the *first* book I would recommend for managers who want to be more effective and for those aspiring to be future leaders!"
—**Daniel K. Saint, PhD, former Partner and Global Practice Leader, Deloitte**

"Jackie and Cheri show us how to change the world one conversation at a time!"
—**Lori Marsee Kuehn, Senior Manager, Global Employee Engagement, General Motors Company**

"We often get stuck seeing the world through a distorted lens. Much may seem broken and unchangeable. Through this lens, doing great work is nearly impossible. That's why—for leaders and managers—reading Cheri and Jackie's book is essential. Their simple techniques help people move from problem to potential, creativity, and continuous growth."
—**Mark Levy, founder of Levy Innovation and author of *Accidental Genius***

"Jackie and Cheri offer the first practical guide to shift our conversations to bring the change we thirst for in ourselves, relationships, and organizations. The simplicity of their practices makes this my go-to resource for working with leaders."
—**Neil Samuels, President, Profound Conversations, and author of *Brilliant: The Heathside Story***

"We create our worlds through conversation. This book shows the difference between conversations that are generative and conversations that hold us back. It illuminates how Appreciative Inquiry can transform personal experience and offer organizations constructive paths forward."
—**Juanita Brown, cofounder of the World Café and author of *The World Café***

"An entertaining and fascinating read! Cheri and Jackie blend stories about personal and organizational conversations with how to frame conversations so people engage and take action. You will never look at your world of conversations quite the same way."
—**Irmgard von Wobeser, family and couples therapist, Centro Psicológico de Cancún**

"Stavros and Torres brilliantly translate Appreciative Inquiry into everyday communication practices for enhancing relationships. Diverse stories about people who have actually applied their ideas make this book interesting, accessible, and highly useful."
—**Diana Whitney, PhD, founder of Corporation for Positive Change and cofounder of The Taos Institute**

"This book is a timely gift. Jackie and Cheri's work has significant relevance for our world of conversations, from individual and group to corporate and international interactions. Their appreciative approach is a welcome addition to the literature on effective communication."
—**Virinder Moudgil, President, Lawrence Technological University**

"Conversation is how we understand each other and build trust. Cheri and Jackie marvelously show us how Appreciative Inquiry supports us. Their framing and flipping exercises are a gift. I will use this book in our workshops."
—**Kathy Becker, President and CEO, Company of Experts, Inc., and CEO, Center for Appreciative Inquiry**

"A great work! A must-read for business managers and teams! Jackie and Cheri show us how we can positively impact people!"
—**Massood Omrani, PhD, Managing Director, CADFEM Americas**

"We carry on conversations in our minds without realizing their influence. Jackie and Cheri show how to make sure there's a positive effect. This book succinctly teaches us to have effective interactions with ourselves and others!"
—**Dan Casetta, Western Region Manager, Cutco Corporation**

"Now is the time for connections through conversations. Jackie and Cheri provide a pathway to lead us past polarity. These two Appreciative Inquiry experts have written a book to help individuals, organizations, and families navigate the choppy waters of differences."
—**Marge Schiller, founder of Positive Change Core**

"This is my favorite book on Appreciative Inquiry! It captures the core concepts in a tight package, explains everything well, and provides techniques you can put to work immediately! To use AI in your work or at home, pick up this gem."
—**Seth Kahan, founder of the Visionary Leadership Academy**

"Jackie and Cheri provide practical ways to use Appreciative Inquiry every day. They show how to solve tough problems, create meaningful dialogue, and build productive relationships using simple practices. My favorite: asking generative questions. Great book!"
—**Jennifer A. Hitchcock, Executive Director, US Army Tank Automotive Research Development and Engineering Center**

"After reading this book, you will be equipped to foster thriving and well-being in your life. This book is brimming with insights, stories, and practical tools. It is a gift to leaders, change agents, and individuals who wish to create positive change! I loved this book!"
—**Jane Dutton, Robert L. Kahn Distinguished Professor Emerita, Ross School of Business, University of Michigan**

"An amazing book with practices to transform your life, family, and organization. Every conversation is an opportunity—a must-read book to deepen connections, strengthen relationships, and change the world for the better."
—**Betsy Crouch and Zoe Galvez, cofounders of ImprovHQ**

"I engage in conversations with stakeholders from the grassroots to local and state levels. This book is a great resource on how to have *conversations worth having*! This is your guide to any conversation in any moment. Keep it close!"
—**John F. Baran, Lead Planner, City of Detroit**

"This book is a gift to the world! It should be read by future leaders, teachers, and parents. The stories moved my heart to understand that conversations make all the difference. I plan to purchase copies for those whom I love."
—**Rose Heinrichs, former elementary and special education teacher**

"This book shifted the way I engage and react in my conversations. It has helped me to express myself genuinely, listen to and understand others, and become a more valuable version of myself—at work and home."
—**Stephanie Schlueter, Manager, Natural View Market**

"This book is for everyone! The authors make it clear, we are our conversations, and it's through our conversations we come alive and make meaning together. It's an easy, delightful read that is uplifting and actionable. The world is ready and waiting!"
—**Robyn Stratton-Berkessel, founder of PositivityStrategist.com**

"I have hundreds of conversations daily. This book reinforces that every conversation builds connection and trust. The authors underscore how the words we use affect others. I now make sure that I have conversations worth having!"
—**Gavin Johnson, Principal, Brighton High School**

"This is a *great* book because it tells you clearly *how* to change conversations to ones worth having. I invite you to read this excellent book and put the concepts into practice."
—**Sue Annis Hammond, founder of Thin Book Publishing**

"Jackie and Cheri share how to transition from downward-spiraling conversations to upward-possibility conversations. For those in the Appreciative Inquiry or positive psychology communities, you will find this book quite useful to your research and practice!"
—**Marrisa Fernando, Director, MMOD Program, Graduate School of Business, Assumption University of Thailand**

"I have lots of conversations with my kids. Most are good—some are not. This book gave me a simple way to communicate more effectively with my children and easily approach conflict."
—**Monica Chester, homeschool mom and nurse**

"Jackie and Cheri teach us to be intentional with our conversations using simple practices to move any conversation away from what we don't want and toward creative possibilities."
—**Jeff Bouwman, Director of Finance and Operations, Western University, and author of *Your Income, Your Life***

"Shared through stories and grounded in science, Jackie and Cheri's book makes a wonderful contribution to the application of Appreciative Inquiry. This book moved me from interest, to hope, to heartfelt awe and empathy!"
—**Sarah Lawrence, founder of Thriving Organisations**

"Our interactions allow organizations to flourish or fade into obscurity. The authors give us a way to host high quality conversations that create an environment that works for all!"
—**Dr. Paul A. Miklovich, Administrator, Cleveland Clinic**

Conversations
Worth Having

Conversations Worth Having

Using Appreciative Inquiry to Fuel Productive and Meaningful Engagement

Jackie Stavros *and* Cheri Torres

Introduction by
David L. Cooperrider

BK

Berrett–Koehler Publishers, Inc.
a BK Life book

Berrett-Koehler Publishers, Inc.
1333 Broadway, Suite 1000
Oakland, CA 94612-1921
Tel: (510) 817-2277   Fax: (510) 817-2278   www.bkconnection.com

ORDERING INFORMATION
Quantity sales. Special discounts are available on quantity purchases by corporations, associations, and others. For details, contact the "Special Sales Department" at the Berrett-Koehler address above.
Individual sales. Berrett-Koehler publications are available through most bookstores. They can also be ordered directly from Berrett-Koehler: Tel: (800) 929-2929; Fax: (802) 864-7626; www.bkconnection.com.
Orders for college textbook / course adoption use. Please contact Berrett-Koehler: Tel: (800) 929-2929; Fax: (802) 864-7626.

Distributed to the U.S. trade and internationally by Penguin Random House Publisher Services.

Berrett-Koehler and the BK logo are registered trademarks of Berrett-Koehler Publishers, Inc.

Printed in the United States of America

Berrett-Koehler books are printed on long-lasting acid-free paper. When it is available, we choose paper that has been manufactured by environmentally responsible processes. These may include using trees grown in sustainable forests, incorporating recycled paper, minimizing chlorine in bleaching, or recycling the energy produced at the paper mill.

ISBN 978-1-5230-9401-1

Library of Congress Cataloging-in-Publication Data
Names: Stavros, Jacqueline M., author. | Torres, Cheri B., author.
Title: Conversations worth having : using appreciative inquiry to fuel productive and meaningful engagement / Jackie Stavros and Cheri Torres; introduction by David L. Cooperrider.
Description: Oakland : Berrett-Koehler Publishers, [2018] | Includes bibliographical references and index.
Identifiers: LCCN 2018003646 | ISBN 9781523094011 (pbk.)
Subjects: LCSH: Interpersonal relations. | Interpersonal communication. | Appreciative inquiry.
Classification: LCC BF724.3.I58 S728 2018 | DDC 158.2--dc23
LC record available at https://lccn.loc.gov/2018003646

First Edition
25 24 23 22 21 20 19 18   10 9 8 7 6 5 4 3 2 1

Book producer and text designer: Steven Hiatt/Hiatt & Dragon, San Francisco
Cover designer: Adam Johnson
Copyeditor: Mark Woodworth
Proofreader: Tom Hassett

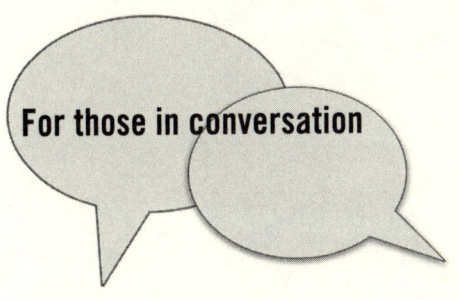

For those in conversation

Contents

Stories

Tables

Figures

Preface

> *Sometimes the greatest adventure is simply a conversation.*
> *— Amadeus Wolfe*

Conversations lie at the heart of how we interact. We are almost always engaged in either internal dialogue or external interaction. But how often are those conversations worth having? We've heard from countless numbers of people who long for positive change in their lives, communities, organizations, and the world. They are tired of meaningless interactions and conversations about change that are negative, drag everyone down, and zap energy—and then nothing happens. They are weary of wasting time on conversations that focus on what's wrong, without producing any actionable results. They are frustrated with the destructive conversations broadcast nationally and globally that fray relationships, pit people against one another, and generate fear and hopelessness. They long for meaningful engagement that builds connection, fuels productivity, and generates positive change.

This book is about those meaningful conversations. It tells how to have conversations that are productive while strengthening relationships and generating possibilities for a future that works for everyone. Conversations worth having energize people. They foster efficiency, fuel meaningful engagement, and generate creative possibilities. They matter because they inspire cooperative action that has a positive impact for individuals, organizations, and communities. We believe that living into our potential begins with these kinds of conversations.

As authors, both of us are longtime practitioners of Appreciative Inquiry (AI), one of the most widely used approaches for fostering positive change in individuals, groups, and organizations. Our journey into AI began in the 1990s when we met David Cooperrider, cofounder of AI. At its core, AI is about discovering the best in people, organizations, and the communities around them. AI is grounded in the notion that we create each moment, and ultimately our social systems, through conversation and shared meaning-making. Appreciative Inquiry is the inspiration of our work as well as the foundation of this book, *Conversations Worth Having*. In its pages, you will learn two simple AI practices and five powerful principles to make almost any conversation one worth having. Rather than heading down a negative path, we show you how to frame conversations in ways that make people you're talking with want to engage and take action. We guide you to ask questions that can change the direction of any conversation, inspiring connection, new knowledge, and innovation. Principles we lay out in the book will influence how you think about your own experiences and challenges, helping you reflect on them more constructively and productively.

Each chapter is built around real-life stories drawn from our personal and client relationships that demonstrate practices and principles that were used to transform both conversations and outcomes. These include primarily applications in the business world, as well as several stories from the realms of education, community change, and family dynamics. We also share the research behind this work, because it is truly evidence-based. From our vantage point, one of the most exciting things about life is the power of a single conversation to make a significant, positive difference. We invite you to join us in creating a positive change in your life and work by engaging in conversations worth having.

We are especially grateful to be working with Berrett-Koehler, whose mission is connecting people and ideas to create a world that works for all. We hope that our contribution to their important work will help to influence positive change on the planet. We invite you to be one of many catalysts who are stimulating conversations to support a world that works for all.

Jacqueline (Jackie) Stavros   *Cheri Torres*
Brighton, Michigan   *Asheville, North Carolina*

jackie@conversationsworthhaving.today
cheri@conversationsworthhaving.today

P.S. We would be grateful if you would share some of your stories with us.

Introduction

We live in worlds our conversations create.
— David L. Cooperrider

"I am struck by the simple fact that my impact as a leader, and even my whole day, goes better when I share my amazement, when we open minds, live into deeper and better questions, and interdependently emerge new things in every conversation . . ."

"Life worth living . . . must be made of affirmation."

These are the words of one of the most remarkable chief executive officers I've ever worked with, arguably one of the greatest, most thoughtful corporate leaders of modern times. In one of its classic cover stories, *Fast Company* called him the Trillion Dollar Man. The article featured Dee Hock's leadership theory and his founding of Visa, one of the largest, most innovative, and successful organizations of the past half-century. Today, Visa has a market value of some $400 billion and annual financial transactions approaching $10 trillion. During Dee's tenure as CEO, the corporation increased its profits by

1

10,000 percent, but more importantly it reinvented the very concept of organization itself. In many ways, it was an early prototype, not a final model, for the more fully human organization we are seeking and even seeing emerge today. The exciting story in Dee's career is his belief in people, which he expresses this way: "The truth is that, given the right circumstances, from no more than dreams, determination, and the liberty to try, quite ordinary people consistently do extraordinary things."[1]

I had the privilege to work with Dee for more than five years. We were uniting the positive power of Appreciative Inquiry (AI) with his concepts of the more fully human organization—a collaborative, intrinsically motivating system capable of liberating the human spirit without reverting to tired, old command-and-control forms of bureaucracy. After years of working with Dee, I began to search for the core of his success. Yes, he was courageous. True, he was tireless. Right, he was an amazing learner. For example, when I visited his home he had just turned his dining room into a massive library spanning the fields of complexity science through the new biology of living systems to the humanities, including many of the classics in art, history, and literature. There were well over 8,000 titles in that "dining room" library, and each one had his underlines, exclamation points, and margin notes. His insatiable love of learning, of course, was a signature strength. And yes, he was skilled as a CEO, with talents in global finance, negotiations, and the future of digital technologies. Yet I still could not put my finger on his mystery. What was that unique difference, that "something more," that made all the difference and made Dee so extraordinary?

It was not until I opened this *very special and graceful book,* by Jackie Stavros and Cheri Torres, that I understood the secret to that CEO's exceptional career and success. Dee Hock had a gift: a Jeffersonian belief in "we the people" and the idea of "organization as community," which I would summarize as this:

Our organizational lives and the lives of others flourish or flounder, one conversation at a time.

For Dee, the difference between success and failure in leadership was all about the art of the "conversation worth having"—precisely the kind that this book describes with such clarity and practicality. Peter Senge, commenting on how Visa was conceived and co-created through literally thousands of conversations and dozens of disciplines, said that the early days of the company "may simply be the best business example of an emerging revolution in organizing."[2]

Change begins with a single conversation.

As CEO, Dee Hock instinctively knew that all the abstract notions of management—corporate culture, strategy formulation, organizational alignment, change management, living the brand, joint venturing, winning the customer, enabling innovation, recruiting top talent, creating atmospheres of aspiring versus fearing, improving connectivity, and scaling up excellence—were accomplished one conversation at a time, with teams, persons, and both small and large system meetings. Dee called "this abundance of interdependent diversity that was the deeper meaning." When I look back at our years of working together, what most stands out was how Dee, when at his best, was a maestro of vital conversations—some of the greatest I've ever been part of. Many of them became defining moments. This experience led me to believe this:

> *Every organization and every life's destiny is a series of defining moments—moments that shape us, change us, and have a huge impact on our development and strategic choices. Our research indicates that almost all of these moments involve the power of vital and caring conversations with significant others.*

After numerous virtual conference calls and telepresence meetings with Dee (not his favorite way of conversing), I recall thinking: "I have never seen a CEO giving so much time and positive energy to each conversation, with such purity of attention, curiosity velocity, mutual inquiry across boundaries; getting everyone engaged like a contact sport; inviting full voice; and modeling the beginner's mind with real listening. Everyone felt appreciated, honored, elevated, and heard."

In one instance, drawing on lessons from the Visa start-up story, we were working with an organization to help its members articulate its body of beliefs, those constitution-like principles that provide the core values for years to come. My job was to apply the mindset of Appreciative Inquiry, an approach that values all voices, seeks to inspire generative theories and possibility thinking, opens our world to new possibilities, challenges assumptions of the status quo, and serves to inspire new options for better living.[3]

Dee called for a conversational process in which a diverse group of all relevant and affected stakeholders would meet and deliberate for three full days, every forty-five days, for an entire year. This schedule provided the time for vital conversations to get at the essence of what matters. Looking back, in a world where relationships are often superficial, this process was astonishing. Because of those inspired conversations, the organization doubled in growth, doubled again, and continues to grow exponentially. So deeply held and valued were its guiding principles that, because of the power of conversations that matter, the organization had the courage to craft one final and concluding principle for the entire global system, with over 850 centers in some 150 countries. This principle stated, "Any individual or organization in this global system can do anything it wants, at any scale, and in any manner—as long as it advances our shared purpose and principles."

This was a radical principle. It asked everyone to be a leader—to build the culture via every conversation. In effect, it told the organization's people that they needed very little traditional supervision. It eliminated the need for a large, expensive, central office hierarchy and thick books on standard operating procedures. It realized that the intrinsic motivation that comes from inspirational beliefs is much more powerful than extrinsic forces. One lesson derived from that principle is highly relevant right now:

> *When you approach each vital conversation as if it could become the most important conversation you might ever have, you can create a positive legacy. How often do we think of our next conversation with this kind of alertness and high anticipation?*

Originally, the prospect of deliberating for three full days, every forty-five days, for twelve months took everyone by surprise. Now, as I look back, I realize it was not the number of days that was important; it was the tough-love message Dee was sending. He was raising the bar on how we conceive of leadership work and think about conversations. In his book that shares the Visa creation story, the word *conversation* is used ten times more than the term *strategic planning*. Conversation is a meeting of hearts and minds. I believe this:

> *When hearts and minds meet, they don't just exchange facts and create atmospheres of hope or despair: They transform them, reshape them, draw different implications from them, engage in new explorations of possibility. Such conversations are literally living systems, living on the edge of chaos and order—like all of life, when it is most alive, busting out all over with pattern and coherence, but also alive with novelty and emergence.*

When you think of conversations worth having, think engagement, interweaving, co-creation, inspiration, respect, illumination, emergence, enriched relationships, trust, empathy, and bringing out the best: *think legacy.*

We live in worlds our conversations create.

Moreover, leadership is a tapestry of both failed and successful conversations that weave the fine threads of our cultures and relationships, budget alignments, customer communities, innovation trajectories, and best places to work into ethical environments where people can thrive and enable their individual and collective greatness to emerge.

On the reverse side of the tapestry, we've also experienced conversations that have caused irreparable damage—destructive conversations. Consider marriages and partnerships where people wish they could replay history and avoid that one unfortunate and explosive conversation that caused a rupture. Consider another life-depleting form of conversation: the boss who begins every meeting by treating the world or the organization as "the-problem-to-be-solved"; where every agenda item is about threats to the business, failure rates, anger about missteps; and where the main life-depleting atmosphere left in the aftermath is fearful and toxic, some combination of disappointment and distance. And, with all of this at stake— each conversation part of a legacy—recall your own schooling. Did you ever take a course on conversations? Not just any kind of conversation, but life-giving ones that serve to open your world to new possibilities, elevate greatness, and build bonds of mutual regard and positive power, not "power over" but "power *to.*"

This book, then, represents a breakthrough in the combined fields of Appreciative Inquiry and Peter Drucker–like strengths-based management, positive psychology, and design thinking. What you hold in your hands is the course you've likely never encountered in only one book but always wanted. *Conversations Worth Having* can change your life at work, certainly. Perhaps even more significant, however, is the difference it can make in creating precious, growth-promoting moments and relationships with significant others, family members, partnerships, and community.

Why my excitement? After all, a handful of books out there today describe courageous conversations, confrontational meetings, conflict resolution, and even "ferocious conversations." And while they, too, show how our lives succeed or fail one conversation at a time, I believe this is the *first* book of its kind to take Appreciative Inquiry's profound promise of positive leadership into legacy-creating conversations.[4] Imagine taking the innovation-inspired tools of design thinking, the strengths-based leadership philosophy of Peter Drucker, the science of positive psychology, and the generative power of Appreciative Inquiry for bringing out the best in people and organizations—and then making all of these accessible as the operating system, even the DNA code, inside every conversation worth having.

The possibility that every conversation can start with a positive frame and end in an even more positive way is the central idea of *Conversations Worth Having*. In pursuing this radical idea, the authors take us into the principles of AI, now being applied at places such as Apple, Johnson & Johnson, the U.S. Navy, Coca-Cola, Verizon, Vitamix, Green Mountain Coffee Roasters, and even the United Nations.

For example, instead of the metaphor that "the-world-is-a-problem-to-be-solved"—which almost automatically triggers a deficit-analytic search into breakdowns, gaps, and root causes of failure and places most of our attention on yesterday—we might consider instead an assumption that organizations are living systems, alive, embedded in "universes of strengths." The most vital conversations, this book's authors have discovered, begin in a wide-angle, valuing way—searching *the appreciable world*, which is always larger than our normal *appreciative capacity*, one where the starting assumption is this:

> *It is not only that we live in a universe of strengths and unlimited human imaginations, but surrounding every change situation we are part of—whether internal to the system or external to the system—there exists the strength combinations and innovation potentials, including consciousness shifts, greater than any organizational challenge or opportunity we will ever face.*

Complexity science describes the concept of "sensitive dependence on initial conditions," which can turn tiny snowballs into mountains of avalanches. We see many of those same dynamics in conversations, right from the fateful moment when they are first framed. Small beginnings can have huge consequences, especially in human systems, which often become what those in the system ask questions about most frequently, authentically, systematically, creatively, and rigorously.

So, *Conversations Worth Having* is not at all about turning a blind eye to anything. Instead, it is about something quite artistic, ever so subtle, seeing *beyond the problem* and inviting a different kind of inquiry or search that creates an empowering environment, one that has a high-strengths density and a prospective, future-forming power. You will witness this different kind of inquiry in the first two stories the authors share in chapter 1, about a large teaching hospital and a failing bank.

This book is built on the authors' relentless optimism, yet it is anything but Pollyannaish. Indeed, in this book, the authors take us into some of the hardest moments any manager, family, business, government, or community might face. *It skillfully provides exactly the right amount of theory for those who want the science of it, but mostly it's about practices you yourself can use and engaging narratives that illustrate and vivify.* The storytelling is honest, heartfelt, and real. You cannot help but reflect on your own life as the authors narrate their own and other transformations.

If you read nothing else, turn to the end of the book for the gripping account of the daughter of one of the authors: It's the true story of a mother and daughter and their response to a young father's harsh and untimely diagnosis of stage four lymphoma. The story, which moved me to tears, was written by the thirteen-year-old daughter, Ally. Courageous Ally teaches us how *Conversations Worth Having* is also about loving and being loved. The bottom line:

> *You learn that in any time, any place, any situation, no mat-*
> *ter what people tell you, conversations matter and that words,*
> *generative questions, and the cognitive power of love—seeing*
> *through the gift of new eyes—can change lives, relationships,*
> *and organizations.*

If you could choose only one inspiring and resource-rich book on leadership as conversation, what do you suppose it would be? For me, the answer is right here in your hands. Jackie Stavros and Cheri Torres—as well as Ally and her father, Paul—have given us a gift. In business, it will strengthen relationships, because the relationship *is* the conversation. In homes and schools, it will help you see and bring out the best in your children and young people—because those, too, are relationships where the conversational ecology is precious and can produce life-defining moments. And when you read this small volume through the lens of your own conversational history, it will likely resonate with something you and many others have experienced:

> *Relationships come alive where there is an appreciative eye,*
> *when we take the time to see the true, the good, the better, and*
> *the possible in each other and our universe of strengths, and*
> *when we use this concentrated capacity to activate conversa-*
> *tions that open our world to new possibilities, elevate collective*
> *genius and purpose, and build bonds of mutual regard and pos-*
> *itive power—not "power over" but "power to."*

In the end, Jackie and Cheri have given us the gift of hope. *Conversations Worth Having* are those that allow us to grow the most and, in the process, also contribute the most. In a world where so many conversations separate us from our vast potentials, may this book change not simply our world but also the world of conversation.

Distinguished University Professor, Case Western Reserve University & Honorary Chair, The David L. Cooperrider Center for Appreciative Inquiry, Champlain College, Stiller School of Business

1

Shifting Conversations

*One great conversation can shift
the direction of change forever.*
— Linda Lambert

Alisha Patel, a senior administrator at a thriving medical center in New England, was surprised at the less-than-stellar patient satisfaction report that was sitting on her desk. Her surprise turned to understanding when she saw which hospital unit this was from. The director of that unit had recently quit because she felt frustrated with the new leadership model and refused to change. Alisha was filling in until a new director was hired.

She sent a copy of the patient satisfaction report to the nurse managers in the unit. She also emailed them an assignment for their next management meeting, which was a week away: *Pay attention. Look for what staff members are doing that contributes to patient satisfaction. Come prepared to share a story of a best practice you've seen during the week.*

The nurse managers were confused when they got the email; one even wrote back, asking if Alisha had made a mistake. "No," she replied, "please look for what's working well and bring your best story next week." This was a dramatic shift from what these nurse managers were used to, and it created quite a buzz. The former director usually read them the riot act, tried to find who was at fault, and demanded they do better, or else. They were glad to see her go!

When the nurse managers met, Alisha acknowledged the team for their quality of care and service to patients. Then she asked about their stories. They each shared a story of best patient care and then together analyzed the stories for strengths and replicable practices. They discovered several unique actions, but mostly there were consistent themes for what created high patient satisfaction. The nurses seemed excited about the ideas. "This was an amazing way to handle our problem, Alisha," one of them exclaimed. "I can't tell you how many meetings we've had that focused on this problem, and nothing ever changed. This was so effective. I know things are going to improve after just one meeting with you!" They left the meeting committed to sharing and implementing the best ideas. They were alive with possibilities!

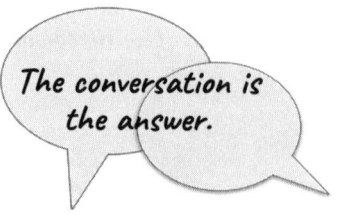

The conversation is the answer.

Alisha smiled confidently as the staff left. She was thinking about the changes that had occurred over the last year. She remembered what it had been like working at the medical center before introducing their new leadership model. They had experienced steady growth in patient services over a three-year period, and, based on that growth, the demands on the staff were having a negative impact on performance, which was evident in their quarterly reports. Patient satisfaction had been steadily declining. Decreasing employee engagement was reflected in unplanned absenteeism and lower retention rates, which made matters worse for everyone. On top of that, patient "throughput" was not optimal, which meant the center lacked the beds they needed to serve the people who needed them most.

All of this negatively affected both the bottom line and employee morale. Everyone felt overworked and stressed. She knew the staff were always striving to provide a high quality of care, but the medical center's growth had become stressful, triggering short tempers, a lack of compassion, limited time for patients, and tension among staff and administration.

Alisha had not always been such an affirming leader. She was responsible for quality, and she lived by the quarterly performance reports. When performance stats were up, she didn't worry; it gave her a chance to focus on other responsibilities. She would send the reports to directors, but she never went out of her way to acknowledge them. She took good reports for granted. When performance stats started declining, it was a different story. She gave the reports all her attention. She spoke face-to-face with directors, and her tone was critical: "These reports are not satisfactory. Every quarter it's the same or worse. You've clearly done nothing to improve!"

The managers would defend the results, saying, "We *have* made changes, but we can't do anything when we are understaffed and people don't show up for work. Some of our staff are already working double shifts to cover for other folks!" "I don't want excuses, I want results," she snapped. "We are doing the best we can," a manager snapped back. "Well, you'll have to do better!" Alisha ended the conversation.

The managers always left demoralized and with no ideas about how to resolve the issue. Alisha's levels of stress and dissatisfaction grew over this period, and it became next to impossible to hide her frustration from her colleagues. Her stress rolled over into her family and nonprofessional life as well. She became short-tempered, negative, and quick to criticize both her kids and her husband. She had fast developed a reputation for being the kind of person she never wanted to be, as a manager, partner, or parent. She realized she was going to have to do something if she wanted things to change. So she began an online search. She was intrigued by the headline of an upcoming workshop she found, about something called Appreciative Inquiry (AI), which promised tools and strategies for strengths-based change at any level—personal, organizational, and community.[1] What caught her attention was this headline:

> The Best Healthcare Clinics in the World
> Are Strengths-Based; Their Performance
> Outpaces All Others!

She read further: *"When we're unable to act with agility, speed, and unity, opportunities are missed and revenue is lost."* It was as if these words were written just for her. In hospitals, she knew, agility and speed can mean the difference between life and death, and lost revenue seemed to lead to financial decisions that negatively affected quality. What convinced her that this was the workshop she needed was a quote from David Cooperrider: *"We change best when we are strongest and most positive, not when we feel the weakest, most negative, or helpless."*[2] She realized she had become negative, focusing on everyone's weaknesses, including her own. Everyone was feeling helpless to turn things around. So she clicked on the registration tab.

During her online training, she learned about the practices and principles of AI. Somewhere in the midst of the week she realized she herself had actually been contributing to the problem at her own medical center. She had dug in her heels and had badgered the staff, without asking any questions or helping to find solutions. She vowed to be part of the solution when she returned.

The first thing she did was to create a positive framework for her next conversation: *More and more, our patients feel highly satisfied with our care.* Then she adopted an attitude of curiosity. She wondered if some of the patients felt highly satisfied. If they were, why? What were their stories? What was the staff who cared for them doing that made a difference? These were the questions she led with at her next staff meeting, and she noted a remarkable shift in the conversation and in more positive outcomes. Alisha felt in awe of how much easier and more effective this approach was. And the proof was in the reports. Quality improved in the next quarter!

A year later, after her recommendation, senior leadership, management, many of the nursing staff, and a handful of physicians had gone through a series of AI workshops that literally gave them the ability to turn their culture around simply by changing their conversations. Alisha thought about her own conversations with staff these days. They were appreciative and inquiry-based, focusing on what they did well and what mattered to everyone: best and heartfelt care, patient recovery, and a place where everyone thrived.

She also realized that her focus of attention had shifted. Instead of seeing the staff themselves as problems, she was seeing their actions as possibilities. Her conversations with them were very different from those she had had a year ago. These were conversations worth having, and the results they pro-duced were creating positive change throughout the medical center.

For example, the Emergency Room staff engaged mem-bers of clinics and urgent care centers in productive conver-sations focused on getting people to use the ER only when needed. They mapped their clinical care strengths and special-ties across the city. They asked questions to inspire possibili-ties and new ways of thinking, as well as ways to work together to help prospective patients choose the right location for care. Such questions included: *What would have to happen for every citizen to know where to go to get quick and reliable care during the day and after hours? How do we make sure transportation is available to move people where they need to go?* The result was a Right-Care, Right-Place plan to help patients learn over time where to go and how to get there. The staffs worked together and developed a system that was delivering *right care in the right places.* Ultimately, this meant the ER team was serving patients who really needed emergency care. It also meant less chaos and crowding in the ER.

What Alisha and most of the staff discovered was that con-versations that were appreciative and inquiry-based fueled pro-ductive and meaningful engagement. These conversations were generating exceptional outcomes. The staff throughout most of the medical center had developed a sense of unity and com-mitment to one another because they intentionally engaged in these kinds of conversations. They routinely thought of inno-vative ways to improve care and consistently put patients—and one another—at the center of all they did. The results spoke for themselves. The work climate changed significantly. This positive vibe made the medical center a place where peo-ple wanted to work. Employee retention improved and staff absenteeism declined. Even when the patient census was high, staff received consistently high ratings that reflected outstanding performance and commitment to excellence.

For Alisha, these positive changes rolled over into her family and personal life just as her frustration had. Alisha found herself initiating more Appreciative Inquiry–based conversations at home, much to the joy of her partner and her children. She found her AI training was every bit as applicable at home and in her community service work as it was at the medical center.

Understanding how appreciation and inquiry enhance relationships as well as productivity and performance is a lesson that Alisha's whole team learned. In our next story about a struggling bank, you will see this point as something that Kamal Amari and Mary Wellington understood well and practiced in their leadership.

The relationship is the conversation.

Kamal and Mary had taken over failing banks and turned them around a number of times. Their success was, in part, due to their capacity for appreciative and inquiry-based conversations. Even when taking over Community One Bank didn't turn out the way they had hoped, great conversations still made all the difference to that bank's employees and customers.

Community One Bank stood as a refuge for the small business owner, first-time homebuyer, and teenager opening a first checking account. Located in the outskirts of Detroit, Community One never focused solely on making money. For the original owners, the goal was to provide quality service in a comfortable environment where people served their neighbors and friends. Early on, they had done well, but times had changed. The bank had been struggling financially for some time. One morning the owners gathered the staff to tell them the bank had been sold.

This news came as a shock to the staff. None of them had been privy to the bank's financial problems. Elizabeth Randall had been with the bank for thirty-eight years when the change in ownership occurred. She had longstanding relationships with her customers, who were more than merely deposit and withdrawal statements. For Elizabeth, her customers were like family. In response to the news, she declared sharply, "I'm not going to work for one of those big banks. They don't care about staff or customers. They only care about making profits!"

When the transition occurred, the former owners introduced Kamal and Mary as experienced bankers with a long track record of turning around struggling banks. "I can't promise you this is going to be easy," Kamal told the assembled staff. "I *can* tell you that if we work together and do this as a team, we can save this bank and continue the tradition that Community One has established over the years. I want to be honest with all of you," Kamal continued. "Given the financial issues with the bank, we will be looking at staffing, overtime, and operating policies and procedures. For the bank to survive, we need to cut costs and meet revenue goals on a budget so that we are financially solvent to take care of you *and* our customers. This means that everyone will have to do more with less."

"I knew it," thought Elizabeth. "They're going to destroy everything we've worked so hard to build here." Kamal and Mary met with each employee individually, and when it was Elizabeth's turn, she prepared herself for the worst. However, the meeting was not at all what she expected. There were no closed doors, and no staff was fired. Elizabeth was completely caught off guard at how their meeting started off.

"Thank you so much for coming to talk to us, Elizabeth," welcomed Mary. "Kamal and I are excited to meet with you. We understand that you have the longest history with the bank and that no one knows this place better than you. We're hoping you'll share your best experiences with us about what makes Community One great. We also want to know: What gives life to this bank and community?"

Kamal and Mary smiled reassuringly in response to Elizabeth's "deer in the headlights" expression. Elizabeth stammered, "You want to know what makes the bank great? But I thought we were losing money!"

"The bank *is* losing money," said Kamal, "and we *do* need to make changes, but we don't want to change what it is about this bank that customers love. We want to learn about what you and the other team members have done to engender such loyalty on the part of this community. We need your experience and knowledge, Elizabeth, and we hope you'll partner with us to turn the bank around."

"Of course I will," Elizabeth agreed. She was stunned at the direction of the conversation. For the next hour, Kamal and Mary peppered Elizabeth with questions, such as: "What do you love most about your job? What wishes do you have for the bank to best serve its customers?" Elizabeth found herself drawn to the magnetic energy of these strangers. They laughed as she regaled them with stories of funny things that had happened over the years. Between their positive questions and these stories, Elizabeth began to remember why she loved her job. Elizabeth also found herself wanting to work with Kamal and Mary in whatever way she could to help the bank succeed.

Over the next eighteen months, the new management worked alongside the staff to make sure everyone was aware of the bank's financial situation and how the changes they were making affected their viability. Naturally, not all the interactions were problem-free. Some difficult conversations occurred. On one such occasion, Kamal asked Elizabeth and another account manager, Ram, to come to his office.

"Elizabeth and Ram," he began, "come in and have a seat. I have a couple of areas that we need to address together. You know we've been working on time management and new accounts over the last month. Elizabeth, it is still taking you too long to open new accounts, and Ram, you don't open many accounts." Elizabeth and Ram each felt a flush of embarrassment, but it vanished quickly because Kamal continued without blaming. Instead of focusing on what they were doing wrong, he acknowledged their strengths and asked them to team up. "Elizabeth, you open the most accounts every month. Ram, you are faster than anyone else at opening accounts. Would you two be willing to work together to combine your areas of expertise to create a fast and effective process for landing new accounts for the bank?"

This led to a great conversation between Ram and Elizabeth. They pooled their strengths and knowledge to develop a replicable process for opening accounts. Elizabeth learned some effective shortcuts on the computer, and Ram learned ways to engage customers and invite them to explore accounts that would be beneficial for them. When they presented their model to Kamal, he seemed quite impressed with their design. He asked them to introduce other staff members to their plan and bring them up to speed with their new process.

Kamal's leadership style had turned a problem into an opportunity to improve things for everyone at the bank, and also to strengthen the leadership capacity of upper-level staff. Elizabeth had come to understand that Kamal and Mary truly had both the employees' and the bank's best interests at heart. Their appreciative, open, and collaborative style of management had converted Elizabeth from skeptic to cheerleader.

Things at the bank were now going extremely well. The bank was not completely out of the red, but they were getting close. Then the 2008 Great Recession struck. To make matters worse, the city of Detroit and all its surrounding communities were hit hard by problems with the automotive industry, the lifeblood of the local economy. This perfect storm negatively affected the bank, and almost overnight the bank went from "on the road to recovery" to "no longer financially viable."

Kamal and Mary gathered the team and announced that a decision had been made to close the bank permanently. Elizabeth and her coworkers were disappointed but not surprised; they understood the economic crisis. Despite the closing, Kamal and Mary pulled off a near miracle. Instead of a massive backlash because of the closing, the whole staff came together and worked as a unified force to close the bank down quickly and efficiently while taking care of the customers. In the end, what could have been a terrible situation ended up as a success. Every customer was counseled on what was best for them, every account was reassigned somewhere else, and every staff member who wanted a job was provided with assistance and training to ensure that they had an opportunity to find alternate work, even at a competing bank.

These two stories illustrate the power of Appreciative Inquiry to foster the kinds of conversations that result in team and organization excellence. AI conversations are worth having because they enliven people, strengthen relationships, unleash creativity, and move organizations forward, fast. They can turn a workplace spiraling into despair into a culture of well-being and innovation. They can pave a pathway to possibility and innovation, even in the face of unforeseen and unfortunate circumstances. Leaders such as Alisha, Kamal, and Mary are skilled at facilitating these kinds of conversations. They know how to draw out the best in people, inspire engagement and commitment, and spark creativity and innovation by using two simple appreciative practices.

Through our twenty-five years of teaching and working with clients using AI, we have learned firsthand the power of positively framing a situation and asking generative questions. AI literally allows people to transform conversations into fuel for productive and meaningful engagement. The material developed in this book reflects our research and practice of AI with our families, organizations, clients, and community groups. Though the names of people and some organizations have been changed, the stories in this book are based on real people. Their experiences provide information that will help you deal with even the most challenging situation, by using two simple practices. This book provides the insight and tools to help you engage in conversations worth having.

If you're thinking "Success doesn't come from putting on rose-colored glasses and just having feel-good conversations," we agree. Yet we assure you that, no matter how complex the challenges or problems you face at work, at home, or in your community, you can have a great conversation about them. We invite you to read on and find out how. You will learn the two AI practices that allow you to consistently turn any conversation into a conversation worth having, and then you'll explore the five AI principles that guide successful practice. You will also learn how to initiate AI conversations at the organizational level, to develop the kind of connections and relationships that foster high-performing teams. You'll come to understand the science behind these practices and learn why holding an attitude of positive inquiry and consistently seeking to contribute value are your best assets for strengthening your relationships with family, friends, and colleagues—and bringing more of what you want into your life. In the next chapter, we begin with the notion that conversation is the foundation of everything we do and create together. *The nature of our conversations determines our well-being and our capacity to thrive.*

2

What Kind of Conversations Are You Having?

The moment of questioning is also the moment of choice, which holds the greatest leverage for effective action and positive change.
— Marilee Goldberg

Conversation is a constant in our lives, whether it consists of our internal dialogue or our interactions with people. We all know these conversations affect us, but we may not realize how much influence they have on our well-being and our capacity to thrive. Not sure about that? Have you ever been in a great mood and having a really good day when a short interaction with someone turned the whole thing sour? Or perhaps you were having a lousy day and a simple conversation suddenly brightened your outlook. In their research, Jeff and Laurie Ford, authors of *The Four Conversations*, actually documented that "the type of conversation you have with the people around you has a profound impact on your experiences, relationships, and accomplishments."[1]

Conversations are almost like breathing. Much of the time, we are unaware of the nature of our conversations and their impact on our experience of being in relationship and in the world. It usually takes a significant (emotional) experience for us to actually step back and reflect on the nature of those conversations. Recall Elizabeth's passion and commitment to the bank and how she felt that those who bought the bank would destroy it. She made a lot of assumptions about what kind of conversation she was going to have in that first meeting. She was stunned when her assumptions turned out to be the opposite of what happened.

The nature of our conversations is far more important than we know. After she got into university, Ming Li, the daughter of one of our colleagues, told her mother that as a child she loved having conversations with her. "I felt connected with you. You empowered me to think and contribute, and those times always stimulated new ideas for me," she said. "They also made both of us feel hopeful and excited about the future. I remember going to school after an early-morning conversation about innovation and renewable energy. I was so motivated by what might be possible! How I might one day contribute to that change." Now, as a young adult, Ming is initiating those kinds of conversations with her friends and professors while earning a degree in environmental engineering.

So, what is it that creates the kinds of conversations worth having? Let's find out by looking at the nature of conversations in general. Conversations have two dimensions: (1) appreciative-depreciative and (2) inquiry-statement, as shown in Table 2.1.

Table 2.1 The Nature of Conversations

The Nature of Conversations	Inquiry-Based	Statement-Based
Appreciative	Conversations Worth Having	Affirmative Conversations
Depreciative	Critical Conversations	Destructive Conversations

The Appreciative–Depreciative Dimension

The first dimension describes the nature of our conversations as either *appreciative* (adding value) or *depreciative* (devaluing). Adding value to a situation, person, or opportunity can show up in a number of ways: sharing ideas, augmenting other people's contributions, naming important factors, advocating for possible actions, acknowledging other people's contributions, suggesting possibilities, pointing out opportunities, responding to questions with new perspectives, and contributing to planning—these are all *appreciative* ways we add value through conversations.

Engaging in such ways strengthens connections, enhances relationships, expands awareness, broadens and builds human potential, adds new knowledge, or moves us toward desired outcomes.[2] Think about times you've collaborated with others to develop creative solutions to a sticky problem or been publicly acknowledged for great work you've done. Remember how these conversations made you feel? Often conversations like these feel good and are energizing. The value-added goes beyond the positive emotions we experience. These conversations literally create an upward spiral of confidence and optimism.[3] They stimulate meaningful engagement and inspire positive action.

By contrast, the *depreciative* dimension devalues a situation, person, or opportunity. This shows up in conversations when someone belittles other people's ideas, criticizes others' contributions, advocates for their own ideas without listening to others, continually points out reasons why things will not work, drives a singular focus, dominates the interactions without making room for others to speak, interrupts or cuts people off, ignores contributions, and complains. Engaging in ways that devalue others actually weakens connections, strains relationships, reinforces assumptions, eclipses human potential, limits possibility, and hinders movement toward desired outcomes. Think back on times you may have argued with someone you cared about or have been on the receiving end of criticism. Did you say things you didn't mean or came to regret later? How did those conversations make you feel?

Depreciative conversations are often described as exhausting and can leave people with low energy, feeling alienated and drained. Research in the field of positive psychology has found that focusing on what is wrong or the negative in an effort to fix something actually narrows our thought repertoire, thereby restricting access to the skills and thinking capacity needed for creativity, critical thinking, and solution-finding.[4] Depreciative conversations can smother creativity, resulting in decreased productivity and disengagement.

The Inquiry-Based and Statement-Based Dimension

In the second dimension, conversations are either *inquiry-based* or *statement-based:* We are either asking questions or making comments. *Inquiry-based* remarks are questions that aim to generate information; reveal hidden assumptions, perspectives, or knowledge; expand awareness; make room for the emergence of possibility or opportunity; deepen understanding; or initiate change. Questions that arise out of curiosity and genuine interest build relationships, connections, and awareness. Such questions add value and are appreciative in nature. Recall a conversation in which someone's questions resulted in your feeling more connected to them or even more inspired to take action. What kinds of questions were asked?

On the other hand, questions can arise from a place of judgment or criticism. Such questions are often rhetorical or pejorative, devaluing people. They are depreciative in nature. Think back to a time when you or someone else asked questions that left you feeling disempowered or critiqued. What kinds of questions were asked in that situation?

Then there are *statement-based* interactions, made up of declarative statements. These comments can add value (affirmative statements) or can devalue (destructive statements). When statements are appreciative, people are saying positive things, responding to questions, and advocating in ways that contribute or point to important facts. Such conversations are valuable and have positive impact on people and situations. Statements that are depreciative in nature often show up as criticism, blame, and general negativity. The seeds of division are sown, leaving little to no room for learning and growth.

Combining these two dimensions—appreciative versus depreciative and inquiry-based versus statement-based—gives us a way to understand the nature of our conversations and their impact. It suggests there are four basic types of conversations or interactions:

1. Conversations that add value through appreciative questions and dialogue: We call these *Conversations Worth Having.*

2. Conversations that add value through appreciative comments and statements: We call these *Affirmative Conversations*. These are also worth having, to a point.
3. Conversations that devalue through depreciative questions and defensive interactions: We call these *Critical Conversations*. These conversations may be worth having, also to a point.
4. Conversations that devalue through depreciative comments and statements: We call these *Destructive Conversations*. These are not worth having.

At the heart of every conversation there is tone and direction: How is the conversation making us feel, and where is the conversation taking us? Many of us find ourselves stuck in conversations that are depreciative in nature. These drag us down and zap energy. Intentionally shifting our conversations to be appreciative and inquiry-based can transform our relationships and workplace outcomes. Think about conversations you've had with family members, friends, colleagues, or your boss. How did you feel after a conversation that you thought was worthwhile? After a critical conversation? A destructive conversation? Or, simply, an affirmative conversation? Which of those conversations had the greatest impact on your sense of well-being or helped you, your colleagues, or your team move forward?

When Kamal asked Elizabeth and Ram to come to his office at the bank to talk about their performance, he could have used several conversational options. The problem was *taking too much time to open accounts* and *not opening enough new accounts*. The tone and direction of the conversation would have been depreciative had he said, "We have a problem. Why is it taking you so long to open accounts? Why do you open so few accounts?" Instead, he stated the problem and reframed it by asking a generative question, inviting his staffers to pool their expertise and co-create a new process for opening accounts at the bank:

> *Elizabeth, you open the most accounts every month. Ram, you are faster than anyone else at opening accounts. Would you two be willing to work together to combine your areas of expertise to have the fastest, most efficient account opening process for the bank?*

This created an appreciative tone that was inquiry-based, with positive direction. Such an approach contributed to Elizabeth's and Ram's motivation to succeed. Their conversation was productive because of that. The result helped them both to improve their productivity, while it also supported excellence for all account managers. Tone and direction influence our health, happiness, relationships, actions, and success in life.[5] Our conversations are worthy of our care and attention. Let's take a closer look at each of these four kinds of conversations and how they show up in our lives.

Conversations Worth Having

Paul put out a text to members of his team on Slack, a cloud-based collaboration application: "Just had a great conversation with @François!" François texted back, "Just took @paul up on offer to drop by Café Sauge Verte and had a fun conversation. He's an interesting guy! I look forward to chatting with him again."

When asked, "What made it a great conversation?" Paul replied, "We were both interested in growing the digital economy in our region, and that's what stimulated our getting together. We didn't know each other and we were wide open to learning new things. François has an interesting background, and, in asking about one another, I learned he has an unusual perspective on opportunities here. In general, I tend to focus on the differences that people bring rather than the similarities. I like that François doesn't agree with me on everything and knows things that I don't. I asked him what he'd like to see happen at a futures institute,[6] and he came up with some ideas that had never crossed my mind. It got me thinking. When he asked why I asked that question, I shared my dream of creating satellite futures events throughout the region. Then we were off and running about possibilities. It was really worthwhile. It was stimulating, positive, and full of potential! And I got to know another techie in our community!"

What made it a conversation worth having was its appreciative tone and positive direction; it was *both* appreciative *and* inquiry-based in nature. Their genuine interest and openness to one another, which created room for each of them to add value to the conversation, made it appreciative. Generative questions were asked about one another's experience and perspectives; this surfaced new ideas and possibilities. The tone was energetic and expansive. The direction spiraled upward as the two men learned about each other and generated possibilities together. Great conversations are generative; they allow for *the creation of new images and metaphors, and they change how people think.*[7] We can recognize conversations worth having by their tone and direction. They are:

- Meaningful
- Mutually enlivening and engaging
- Geared to generating information, knowledge, and possibility

- Solution- or outcome-focused
- Uplifting and energizing
- Positive
- Productive

The appreciative, inquiry-based conversation between Paul and François resulted in a new friendship, the surfacing of diverse perspectives and skills, the generation of ideas and possibilities, and the energy for moving forward.

We've all participated in conversations worth having, which by their nature are appreciative and inquiry-based interactions. They are typically rich and deep. You know you're in a great conversation when you are energized and filled with positive emotions, images, and actions. Your thinking and creativity broaden and build. Your awareness expands and triggers insight. In the workplace, such conversations fuel productivity, performance, engagement, and satisfaction, all of which promise to support excellence.[8] In communities, new futures are made possible. At home, such conversations create strong family bonds and support the potential of family members to thrive.[9]

Unfortunately, this is not the nature of many of the conversations we engage in day to day, nor is it the nature of most conversations being broadcast in the media. Too often, at home, at work, on social media, in the news, and in TV programming, we engage in or witness critical and destructive conversations. You might think, "Well, that's just human nature." But recall the impact of such conversations on the medical center's ability to thrive. Over time, depreciative conversations destroy our sense of well-being and eclipse our potential to contribute. They negatively affect workplace engagement, team performance, productivity, and organization success. Furthermore, such conversations fray our relationships, deplete our energy, waste time, and depress our will to try, much less excel. Such conversations affect us physically, mentally, and emotionally, draining our potential for well-being.

If it is "just human nature" to focus on the negative or to be critical, some might say we should simply resign ourselves, even though we know that this depletes us across the board. On the other hand, we also know that human nature is adaptable and habits are flexible; so the best response is not resignation but intentionality. We can learn to shift our conversations. Before diving into how to do this, it is valuable to understand the nature of the other three kinds of conversations: critical, destructive, and affirmative.

Critical Conversations

The boss ordered the team into her office, and it was clear she was not happy. Stefan looked down and sighed as his shoulders slumped at the boss's words. "Who the h!@*! submitted this to the Executive Committee?" she asked. "Does this look professional to any of you?" she snapped as she threw the ten-page report across her desk. Stefan had not thought it was ready to send, but she had demanded the report be sent no later than yesterday, and she would not entertain a conversation about a later date. As team lead, Stefan spoke up: "I told you it wasn't ready, but you said to send it anyway."

"Oh, so now it's *my* fault?" she barked.

"I'm not saying it's your fault, I'm just saying I tried to tell you we weren't ready," said Stefan.

"So why *weren't* you ready? Is someone not pulling their load? This isn't the first time your team has missed deadlines. Now the VPs are breathing down my neck, thinking we don't have what it takes to do this job."

"In all fairness," Stefan said, defending himself and his team, "this is an exceptionally qualified team. As usual, we didn't have the time or the equipment to move any faster in getting the results you wanted. We're at the mercy of our equipment and the process. Once we get things set up, all we can do is wait." The rest of the team was silent, staring at their feet and feeling uncomfortable. The boss dismissed them with a wave of her hand. "Get back to work, and let me know how soon you can get a *professional* report ready for me. This time I want to see it *before* it goes out!"

The tone and direction of this conversation are quite different from those of the previous one. The boss's depreciative questions drained the energy out of the room. The conversation was a volley back and forth between defense and offense, attack and deflection. The interaction eclipsed any sharing of valuable information that might have generated productive solutions. It lowered morale among team members and added another brick to the wall between the boss and her employees. The team left the conversation knowing only that they didn't live up to their boss's expectations and yet not quite sure how to move forward. This conversation hindered creative possibilities for delivering on desired outcomes; it was a matter of starting over or waiting for the process to be completed.

We've all been part of such conversations, sometimes as the critic and sometimes as the one critiqued. Many times the critic does not see herself as being critical. In intimate relationships, critical-sounding conversations seem to be part of the territory. For example, a seemingly benign kitchen remark such as, "Sweetheart, why don't you use just one pan? It will be so much easier and less work in the end" can launch a cascade of undesired results and friction. The person saying this is merely trying to be helpful. The other person, however, depending on past interactions, assumptions, and their own state of mind, can feel criticized and may snap back, "Why do I have to do it *your* way?"

Judgment and criticism lie at the core of a critical conversation. The person being asked the question(s) typically experiences a negative emotional response: defensiveness, fear, shame, unworthiness, anger, or disempowerment. Depreciative questions often reflect an unequal power dynamic (boss–subordinate, parent–child, teacher–student, more experience in the kitchen versus less experience in the kitchen), where the person being asked the question experiences being "one-down." Such deficit-based questions negatively affect the mood and confidence of people.[10] These kinds of interactions typically lead to disengagement and lowered productivity.

Occasionally, critical conversations *can* be valuable and productive. Examples of this abound in our organizations, schools, and families. Root-cause analysis, which is a problem-solving method for finding the root cause of a problem, can surface an easy fix. Critical feedback can motivate change, but it will not sustain it. Arguments between couples can bring issues out in the open that need to be aired. All of these are examples of critical conversations with positive outcomes. Usually, getting to that outcome does not feel good, though the outcome is nonetheless positive.

Critical conversations have the ability to be effective when balanced with strong relationships that have formed as a result of predominantly appreciative conversations. Research shows that the best results for teams and relationships stem from a 6:1 relationship (six positives to one negative).[11] Over time, if critical conversations dominate the conversational landscape, they eventually weaken relationships, limit potential, and eclipse generativity. In effect, they become destructive conversations. When the ratio falls below 3:1, things begin to fall apart.[12]

Destructive Conversations

Shane and Jean-Luc were standing around the coffee machine. "If I have to listen to Claudia talk about her sales goals one more time, I'm gonna hit something," said Shane in exasperation. "I know what you mean," added Jean-Luc. "She's so oblivious to how she makes the rest of us feel."

"Yeah, well, she didn't get all those sales on her own. I'll bet the manager steers some of them her way. You've seen how they look at each other, haven't you?" Shane insinuated.

"Whoa, I didn't know that! That's not fair," fumed Jean-Luc. "That annoys me. To think I have to put together a proposal with her tomorrow! I will have to be careful with her and keep my cards close to my chest. She'll probably make me do all the work, and then she'll take all the credit."

You can see where this conversation is going, and also how it will influence Jean-Luc's ability to work with Claudia the next day. This is a destructive conversation with no chance of a positive outcome. It creates or reinforces differential power dynamics, generates a negative tone, and creates roadblocks for progress toward desired outcomes. The conversation is full of statements that devalue Claudia, her work, and the manager. Without her even being present, the relationship between Claudia and her two colleagues has been fractured. Jean-Luc has been set up to anticipate a negative interaction in which he loses. Unless Jean-Luc realizes the destructive nature of his conversation with Shane, his interaction with Claudia the next day is likely to be critical or destructive. There is little chance they will have a highly productive and meaningful engagement.

For those in an intimate relationship, a critical or passive-aggressive question such as "Why do you always have to leave your stuff lying around?" can trigger a destructive conversation between partners: "You are such a nag!" "I wouldn't have to nag if you'd put your stuff away!" "It's my house, too, and I like my stuff where it is! You are such a control freak!" "I'm not trying to control, I just like a house that's clean and neat. It's better feng shui; energy gets caught up in clutter." Rolling his eyes, "Oh jeez, now it's feng shui!"

This couple is talking past one another—full of judgment and criticism, denying one another's value in the process. The conversation is loaded with blame, name-calling, and fault-finding, which then trigger attack-and-defend stances. Not only are such conversations *not* worth having, they are toxic. They destroy both relationships and the potential for excellence. When such conversations are the norm, they are actually predictive of low-performance teams and even divorce.[13]

You can tell you are in a destructive conversation because it drains life and energy from those involved. It spirals downward, augmenting negative feelings. People on the receiving end do not feel valued and do not contribute value. No one feels good about the dynamic. Once defensiveness is triggered, statements become reactionary, fueled by negative emotions that tear down and narrow both creativity and critical thinking. Relationships grow more and more strained, and over time trust erodes. Just as they did at the medical center, such conversations create a toxic environment. Such a climate results in lower productivity, disengagement, dissatisfaction, and loss of connection. If the situation continues, relationships disintegrate. Organization teams fail to perform well. Employees mentally check out, quit, or form cliques that generate divisiveness. Families can even fall apart. These destructive conversations often take the form of any of the following:

- General deficit-based narrative: blaming, disempowering, claiming authority, or otherwise minimizing the worth of others
- Arguing or debating, without listening to one another
- Bullying
- Commanding and controlling
- Strict advocacy, with no inquiry into what others are thinking

The tone of destructive conversations feels bad and stimulates negative emotions. The direction often sits in spin cycle, going nowhere. Instead, the negative tone amplifies. Almost the opposite is true of the fourth and final type of interaction: the Affirmative Conversation.

Affirmative Conversations

A high school teacher affirms, "Samantha and Tamir, you've done an excellent job on your project! It's clear you both put in a great deal of time, and you met the criteria for earning an A. I would like you to present your project to the class tomorrow."

"Thanks," said Samantha and Tamir in unison. "You helped us a lot; we could never have done such a good job without all your support," added Tamir.

"Well, that's what I'm here for," the teacher replied. "All I did was give some suggestions and leads on where to look for things. You both did all the hard work and put it together in such a polished final product. You should be very proud of your work!"

This is one form of affirmative conversation. The tone augments positive emotions and good feelings, yet it is nondirectional. The impact it has on the emotions can nonetheless inspire forward movement and motivate positive action. Another form of affirmative conversation is mutual advocacy: You share your ideas and others share theirs. Such conversations typically transition into one of the other types of conversations. If debate, criticism, and argument arise, you've moved into a destructive interaction. By contrast, a conversation worth having emerges if people in that conversation seem genuinely curious about one another's points of view or how their ideas might come together. As soon as questions are asked that generate new knowledge or invite creativity, the interaction becomes a conversation worth having. Affirmative conversations center on the following:

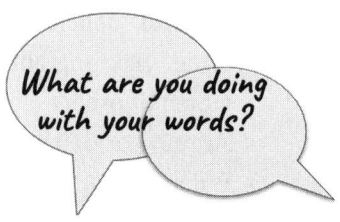

- Genuine (mutual) admiration
- Acknowledgement
- Feedforward[14]
- Motivation/encouragement
- Positive advocacy

The difference between a conversation worth having and an affirmative conversation is palpable. The latter, like the one Samantha and Tamir had with their teacher, simply feels good. It reinforces positive relationships and encourages excellence. Yet it lacks the vibrancy and dynamic energy of a conversation worth having. Engaging in affirmative conversations is important because they foster a climate that favors potential and creativity. On their own, however, these conversations are not sufficient to generate new knowledge or innovation.

Over time, engaging in affirmative conversations may be experienced simply as "being nice." Without generative questions being asked, affirmative conversations can result in a friendly but superficial environment where no real learning and growth take place. We may like and appreciate one another after such conversations, but we really don't achieve the same depth of relationship or find possibilities for the future that develop when we inquire deeply together.

Excessive or insincere affirmative conversations backfire. Inauthentic appreciation can create a toxic environment over time. These interactions may show up as "talking nice" to someone's face while making negative comments behind their back, or using affirmation and praise to gain something of value only for oneself. Such expressions and manipulations become self-evident to everyone involved, except perhaps the person perpetrating them. Over time, these are experienced as destructive conversations.

Take a few minutes and think about times you have been engaged in each of these types of conversations in your personal and professional life. Where did your conversations take you (direction), and how did they feel (tone)? Those two questions are key indicators of the kind of conversation you are having. In the next chapter, as promised, we will introduce you to two simple AI practices that will allow you to intentionally fuel productive and meaningful engagement.

3

Two Simple Appreciative Practices

Creating a positive future begins in human conversation. The simplest and most powerful investment any member of a community or an organization can make is to begin with other people as though the answers mattered.
— William Greider

We saw in chapter 1 how Alisha at the medical center changed the direction and tone of her conversations simply by varying her frame of reference and asking a question that altered everything. Her frame shifted from *employees as problems* to *employee ideas and actions as possibilities*. From this new frame of reference, a different set of questions emerged, inspiring solutions and more effective interactions than previous critical conversations. These questions helped her staff focus on what was working and what could be working better. The answers enabled them to replicate success and create new possibilities.

Likewise, Kamal and Mary at the bank intentionally framed their first meeting with Elizabeth to set the stage for appreciative tone and positive direction. Inviting her to share her best experiences about what gives life to the bank and the community resulted in a conversation worth having.

The two practices Alisha, Kamal, and Mary applied were the Appreciative Inquiry practices of positive framing and generative questions. It can be difficult to separate these practices in action, because they weave together to create conversations worth having. Nonetheless, they are in fact distinct. It is worth understanding how each is practiced and contributes to productive and meaningful interactions. Each practice can alter the tone and direction of any conversation. You can begin with positive framing and then ask generative questions, or you can start with a generative question that naturally creates a positive frame, or you can ask a generative question in the midst of a negative interaction to turn that conversation around.

Positive Framing

Remember when Kamal called Elizabeth and Ram into his office? He wanted to talk with them about how long it was taking to open accounts and how few were actually being opened, respectively. He could have directed the conversation toward each of them and used a critical tone and direction. Instead, he framed the conversation around working together to create a model for *rapid new-account generation*. This was the desired outcome. It made it easy to invite Elizabeth and Ram to help figure out how to do that. Kamal brought a positive frame to that conversation. Positive framing is not only about focusing on the positive.[1] It is also about focusing attention and action on *where we want to go* or *on what it is we want more of.*

To inspire a conversation worth having, use positive framing, which creates a desirable focus. A positive frame draws people in and inspires curiosity, imagination, and interest. For examples of positive framing, see Table 3.1.

Table 3.1 How Positive Framing Draws People In and Inspires Engagement

A Positive Frame . . .	Inspires Curiosity, Imagination, and Engagement
Our employees feel valued, and each of them collaborates with a highly productive team.	• *I want to work there! What company is this?* • *How do you know employees feel valued?* • *What contributes to feeling valued?* • *What makes them productive?* • *How can we do more of what you do, so our employees have the same experience?* • *Imagine what it would be like if that were the case here!*
Employees look forward to their quarterly performance reviews.	• *Really? Why? What goes on in your reviews that makes employees like them?* • *What would have to happen for my employees to look forward to these conversations?*
Let's plan our vacation so each of us feels like it was our best vacation yet!	• *That sounds awesome. I want to spend lots of time in the water!* • *Does it matter what kind of water? Because I'd love to go to the beach.* • *How does everyone feel about seeing a few shows?*
Our students thrive, regardless of whose class they are in.	• *How is that possible?* • *What do you mean by "thrive"?* • *What do you do to help them thrive?* • *How do you get all teachers and students on board?* • *How can we spread this to all our schools?* • *I want my children enrolled in your school!*
In our town, we're talking across all sorts of divides: racial, gender, and political. And we're finding ways we can all live together well.	• *How did you do that?* • *How did you get people to the table?* • *What do you talk about?* • *We're trying to do that but we keep bumping up against fear and resentment. How did you get beyond that?* • *Who helped lead this?*
Imagine that after five years we could say that we've made great strides in reducing our environmental footprint each year.	• *I'm up for that!* • *Where shall we start?* • *My department has already been trying to do this. I can share what we've been doing.* • *We may need to make some policy changes. Anyone interested in focusing on those?* • *How do we get people engaged and committed?* • *What can the city/management do to set a high standard?* • *How are we going to measure success?* • *I wonder what other cities/organizations have done?*

You can apply positive framing to virtually any situation, conversation, evaluation process, meeting agenda, planning process, interview, or interaction. You can do this at the outset of a conversation, or you can shift a conversation if you realize it's depreciative. No matter what the situation or with whom you are talking, you can frame (or reframe) the focus in a way that inspires a conversation worth having. The dynamics of our conversations is always influenced by our focus of attention (or frame). Mark's story illustrates this effect.

Mark, a mid-level manager in a Fortune 100 company, was preparing for a tough conversation with an employee who was very good at her job. There was one major problem: She was routinely late for their weekly meeting and sometimes missed deadlines. He and his mentor were talking about how he might frame this conversation.

Our framing and questions are fateful.

Mark was smiling as he mused, "Before you taught me the two basic AI practices, I would have seen Melissa as the problem. I probably would have said something like, *'We have a problem; you are always late and miss deadlines. You have to change.'* I would have framed a critical or possibly a destructive conversation and asked critical questions. I now know *exactly* how that would have played out!"

His mentor nodded and asked, "So, how *are* you going to frame your conversation with Melissa?"

Mark replied, "Well, I'm still not totally sure, which is why I wanted to talk with you. Here's what I'm thinking about doing: Instead of making her the problem, I'm thinking about focusing on a high-performance team and framing the conversation around behaviors that affect the team and our

performance. I thought I would start by saying, *'You do excep-*
tionally good work, and your input is very important to our team's
success. Because of that, it's really vital that everyone arrive on
time, if not a few minutes early, to our meetings and also to make
deadlines on time. When you are late, it affects all of us. What
ideas do you have for how we plan and schedule things that could
resolve this?' What do you think?"

Mark's mentor smiled and said, "I think you are going to
have a productive conversation." As he left, he added, "Remember to think about your own role, as well."

It's important to note that Mark was not going to skirt the
problem; rather, he was planning to address it head on and
invite Melissa to be part of the solution, just as Kamal did
with Elizabeth and Ram. The practice of positive framing has
allowed Mark to maintain good relational dynamics with his
employees while resolving issues that are negatively affecting
overall team performance. The result is a department that has
a strong sense of well-being and a team that is flourishing. In
this particular situation, Melissa may still feel bad because the
problem is the result of her actions, but the focus is on the
desired outcome, not herself. It allows her to share potential
problems that may be impeding her ability to be on time. New
information has the potential to surface solutions.

Positive framing is about intentionally shaping a conversation that invites engagement and produces positive outcomes.
This applies at work, at school, at home, in our community
outreach, and even when we have internal conversations with
ourselves. We always recommend that you begin where you
are when you start practicing positive framing. If you're like we
once were, and also like most of our clients, you'll start with
a problem-oriented or negative focus of attention. When this
is the case, simply reframe the focus. A process for reframing

a conversation, task, or topic can begin with a technique we call *flipping*.[2] It's a simple way to reframe the depreciative to the appreciative.

Flipping

After his mentor left, Mark spent a bit more time thinking about the positive frame he wanted to use and reflecting on how his actions might have contributed to the problem. He had not considered that he himself might somehow be playing a role in Melissa's being late. Just considering that he might own some responsibility here made him feel more open and less critical of her. He thought through the flipping process so as to shift his original depreciative frame to an appreciative one. He took the time to get very clear on the impact Melissa was having and what the outcome of her being on time would be for the department. His mental process went something like this:

- What is the problem? *Melissa is routinely late and misses deadlines.*
- What is the positive opposite of the problem? *Melissa is routinely on time and meets deadlines.*
- What would be the impact if Melissa were on time? What is the desired outcome? *The team has a strong sense of cohesion: Performance improves, while trust, mutual respect, and collaboration are solid. All these help us sustain excellence.*

Notice that the steps to reframing from problem to positive frame are stimulated by generative questions, especially the move from positive opposite to the new frame. These questions generate both a new perspective and a broader context for the conversation. The new frame typically inspires curiosity.

For Mark, reframing expanded his awareness and gave him the broader context for why it was important for team members to be on time.

It also caused him to wonder if there were other things that could be done to build cohesion, and how he could better contribute to that. Were there things he might have done to set the stage for success? By not doing them, had he set Melissa up for failure? That consideration influenced his state of mind and openness when Melissa arrived for their one-on-one meeting. Mark started the conversation by saying, "Melissa, I want to ensure that we have a strong team grounded in trust, responsiveness, mutual respect, and cohesion because I think it will allow us to be remarkably successful together. What do you think?" Melissa replied with some hesitation, as she wasn't sure where this was going, "I agree; I hope I am contributing to that."

Mark responded, "I hope I'm doing all I can to contribute to that as well, but I'm not so sure I am. I'm glad you and I are on the same page with this. You do excellent work, and your input is very important to our team. You certainly are contributing to our success. I am noticing something that I'd like to address, and I need your help. I'm sensing that people are getting frustrated in meetings when you're not there or when something isn't turned in on time. It means they can't move forward because you have important information to share. You are a valued member of this team. I'm afraid that their frustration will build over time and affect the team's trust and cohesion. Do you have some ideas about how we can make sure we stay a strong team? Is there something I need to be doing that would make that possible?"

Melissa felt embarrassed, but it seemed that Mark was open to her input. So she shared, "The meetings I'm late for are scheduled at 8 a.m. on Wednesdays, and I have a very difficult time getting here on time on that day. That's the only day I drop my son, Connor, at day care. All other days, my husband takes him, but he can't on Wednesdays. If we could schedule our standing meeting for 8:30 or 9 a.m., or for any other day, I can assure you I'll be on time."

Mark looked shocked, then asked, "Is that *all* it will take? Surely, we can find another time. We'll reschedule at our next meeting." He realized he'd never asked people about the timing of the meeting.

"And, about deadlines," added Melissa, "I hate it when I miss deadlines, too; that's not the kind of reputation I want to be known for. I'll admit sometimes I'm just late, and I need to work on being timely. However, there are times when members of the team set deadlines without understanding what it will take to meet those deadlines. I should probably speak up when I know it's not likely I can meet that deadline, but I feel like I'll be letting the team down if I don't try."

Recognizing that his own leadership played a role in this dynamic, Mark responded, "I want you to know that each of us owns a piece of the responsibility here. I need to take some ownership for not involving employees in decisions about meetings, and the team needs to make sure that whenever deadlines are set, everyone affected by those deadlines will be in on the conversation. I will take responsibility for addressing this at our next meeting. For your part, Melissa, in the future, please speak up if you think that a deadline is unrealistic, even if it's been set and if you were not present at the time. Doing that actually makes you a better team player. Either we can change the deadline or the team can help brainstorm how they might support you in meeting that deadline. Will that work for you?"

You can readily see that positive framing turned a potentially destructive conversation into a productive and meaningful one. To practice this yourself, use our simple three-step *flipping* process. This is shown in Figure 3.1.

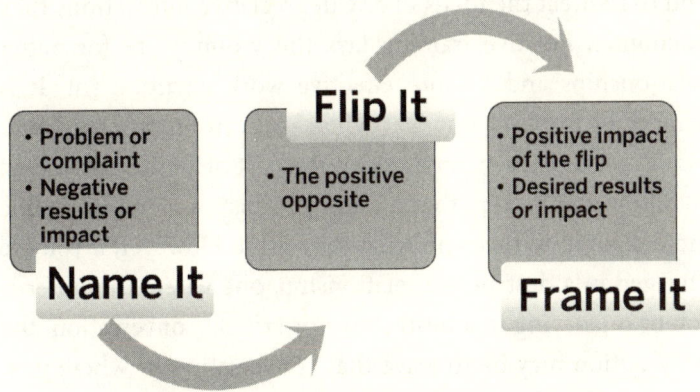

Figure 3.1 Flipping: Framing a Conversation Worth Having

- Step 1: **Name It.** What is the problem, complaint, or the thing you don't want?
- Step 2: **Flip It.** What is the positive opposite, the thing you *do* want?
- Step 3: **Frame It.** What is the positive impact if the flip were to be true? What is the desired outcome?

When reframing a conversation, it's vitally important to have an open mind, because *flipping* typically takes us in a new direction. Reflect on the reframe to make sure that it will resolve or dissolve the original issue. For example, Melissa's tardiness dissolves as a problem when she and her boss discover that the real issue is scheduling, and her late work is resolved in their agreement that in future she will speak up about deadlines. For this reason, it's beneficial to reframe outcomes so that solutions can involve ideas or people other than those originally thought to be part of the problem, including yourself.

This simple practice is helping thousands of people to optimally set the tone and direction of their conversations and to redirect the focus of any depreciative interactions they encounter. Positive framing lays the groundwork for better relationships and a more effective work environment. It is important to point out that while you can reframe any conversation, it takes willingness on the part of all those involved to follow your lead in that reframing. Most of the time, people are delighted to focus on what they want. However, if you are engaged in a destructive relationship, one where the other is intent on staying in a destructive or critical conversation, the only option may be to leave that conversation or where possible add others to the conversation. Find a trusted colleague or friend to have an Appreciative Inquiry–based conversation about how you can take needed action either to keep yourself safe or to effectively mitigate the negative dynamic.

As we mentioned at the outset, positive framing and generative questions are woven together in an appreciative and inquiry-based interaction. As you read earlier, these techniques are even interwoven when developing a positive frame. Let's take a closer look at what these kinds of questions are, and how they support conversations worth having.

Generative Questions

This second practice invites you to adopt an attitude of curiosity. When we are curious, we naturally ask generative questions. Our colleague Gervase Bushe best describes generativity as "the creation of new images, metaphors, or physical representations that have two qualities: they change how people think so that new options for decisions and actions become available to them, and they stimulate compelling images people act on."[3] In other words, generative questions do the following:

- They make room for diverse and different perspectives: *How do you see it?*
- They surface new information and knowledge: *How did they manage this process at your previous plant?*
- They stimulate creativity and innovation: *What might be possible if we merge marketing and development?*

When dealing with any issue, even difficult ones, generative questions result in conversations that create trust, positive energy, and the transformative power to move the system forward in a positive direction. Generative questions focus on the best of what *is* and what *might be*. The result: new ways for solving complex problems and compelling images for collective action.

In the following story, Monica is able to change the conversational dynamic with her son by using generative questions. Monica had been in the midst of a recurring argument with her teenage son, Aiden. She was tired of the same old interaction that never produced a way forward. Aiden wanted to borrow the car over the weekend to go "do things" with his friends, and Monica didn't like the idea of his joyriding, with the possibility of getting into trouble. Their critical conversations had created a rift between them, which saddened Monica, but she didn't know what else to do.

Suddenly, in mid-conversation, it occurred to her she could use the practice she's learned at work for shifting the tone and direction of a conversation. When Aiden started to reiterate the argument, Monica held up her hand, paused, and said, "I really do understand why you want the car, and I hope you understand why I'm worried for your safety and well-being. So, how can we have a more productive conversation? How can we come to some agreement that allows you to get the car and me to feel comfortable that you'll make good decisions, even if your friends are pressuring you?"

Aiden was stopped in his tracks. This time it was his turn to pause, and then they began a brand-new conversation that promised to be worthwhile . . . and it was. Monica's question allowed Aiden to let his mom know that he did understand. He shared that sometimes he was glad he hadn't been allowed to have the car because of where his friends ended up. But other times, he had missed out on experiences he wanted to have. At those times, he felt she was being overprotective. On hearing that, she realized she hadn't even considered that part of the stalemate might be her own refusal to let go. Monica and Aiden eventually arrived at an agreement to start small and keep expanding car privileges as trust and confidence grew between them.

Monica shifted the conversation out of critical debate and into a conversation worth having, first by reframing the situation and then by asking a generative question. This simple action shifted the tone and direction of the conversation. It allowed both of them to step back, reflect for a moment, and be more open and honest, which shifted the outcome of their interaction. This is one of the most valuable practices you can develop for building strong relationships, expanding the potential of a group, surfacing possibilities in the face of challenges, and rapidly moving toward desired goals.

Asking generative questions is an essential practice for stimulating productive conversations and inspiring engagement. Generative questions that deepen understanding among people strengthen their relationships. These questions stimulate creative thinking, inspire hope, and create momentum to move forward. This is true for families as well as organizations. It is even true for resolving global issues, as was the case for Jerry Sternin.

In the 1990s, Jerry worked for Save the Children, an international nongovernmental organization working on behalf of children's well-being. The government of Vietnam asked Save the Children to help it with childhood malnutrition in the south of the country.[4] Jerry landed in Vietnam and was promptly told by the Foreign Minister that not everyone was pleased he was there, and that he had only six months to make a difference. Any thoughts about doing traditional problem solving, such as achieving clean water, setting up educational programs on nutrition and sanitation, and eliminating poverty, were clearly not going to work. Jerry pondered a generative question: *I wonder if there are families where the children are thriving?*

Innovative solutions can be found in what's already working.

This question inspired Jerry to bring together teams of mothers from rural communities to help him answer it. He asked them to weigh and measure all the children, in hopes of finding some children that were not malnourished. Meanwhile, he talked with as many people in the community as he could to discover their eating norms. He found consistencies: Mothers did the food preparation, families ate twice a day, and children ate with adults and fed themselves. The children ate soft, clean food (no crustaceans), and if they were sick, they did not eat. Meanwhile, the data the mothers gathered showed that there were, in fact, small pockets that represented exceptions to the norm in the community: There were children of very poor families who were healthier and bigger than the standard.

Jerry asked another generative question: "Is there something the mothers of these children are doing that is making the difference?" Observation and conversations with these mothers surfaced important differences; they did not follow the cultural norms. In these families, children ate the same amount of food, but it was spread out over four meals. If the children did not eat on their own, their mothers fed them. These children were served small shrimp and crabs as well as sweet-potato greens, which were considered a low-class food. In addition, when children were sick, they ate. The difference in diet was significant: These children were receiving more protein and vitamins on a daily basis. They had discovered a native solution to the problem of malnourishment. So Save the Children implemented a program for mothers with healthier children to teach other mothers in their community how to feed their children in a more beneficial way. In six months, they made a positive difference in the well-being of these families—and discovered a solution that could be spread.

Jerry had challenged ordinary ways of thinking about the problem. Instead of asking questions about fixing the structural and cultural issues related to malnutrition, he looked for positive deviance.[5] The solutions were already present in the community. He discovered them by asking generative questions.

Sometimes we find ourselves in the midst of a critical or destructive conversation because no one is paying attention to the nature of the conversation. Shifting a negative conversation to a positive one can be initiated by using generative questions. In the following story, you will see how Gabriela asks a simple question that flips a negative conversation into an appreciative one.

Gabriela, an organization development consultant, attended a reception on the last evening of an AI workshop. She was talking with the provost of a large midwestern university about a new project it was undertaking that promised to engage students and improve student learning outcomes. The provost was complaining, "We have invested so much time and money in this powerful new learning management system, and I just can't get the faculty on board. It's so frustrating, especially for students. I sometimes wonder whether they simply don't get how beneficial this is."

Inquiry and change are not separate movements.

Gabriela had been listening and commiserating. She had her own viewpoint about academicians, which lined up with what he was saying. She added to this depreciative conversation by asking, "That's pretty typical of faculty, isn't it?" and "Why are they always so resistant to anything new?" Suddenly, Gabriela realized that she was asking depreciative questions, which were keeping this critical conversation going. She thought, "Okay, let's give this AI approach a test drive. We'll see if I can change this conversation just by asking a simple question to flip the focus."

The next time the provost paused, she asked, "Are there any faculty who are on board with what you are trying to do?" Before she even completed the sentence, the provost brightened, stood taller, smiled, and with enthusiasm and a completely different tone declared, "Oh yes, the College of Management is completely on board! They've adopted this wholeheartedly!" Then he went on to describe all the things the faculty were doing and the successes their students were having. But Gabriela wasn't listening any more. She was in awe of how easy it had been to shift the conversation.

All Gabriela did was ask a generative question about the positive opposite of what the provost was saying. Her question literally flipped the conversation *in the moment*.[6] This is one of the simplest tactics for shifting a conversation from depreciative to appreciative. These stories are only a few of the many client stories we have gathered that demonstrate the power of positive framing and generative questions. These two simple AI practices shift our attitude, make room for innovation, and invite people to show up, engage, and participate. When people are invited to share their knowledge and ideas, it encourages everyone to stay open and listen. This broadens and builds our access to critical thinking and creativity.[7] When Monica asked her son to help create a solution that would work for both of them, Aiden stopped advocating for himself and opened up to his mother's needs, as well. Such framing and questioning expand possibilities for action, increase the odds for new knowledge and innovative solutions, and pave a path for flourishing.

Asking a generative question starts with curiosity and an open mind. We suggest that this begins with reflecting on our *own* frame. Where is *our* focus of attention? Are we open to *any* answer, or is there an agenda or a set of assumptions behind our question? Recall Alisha before she brought AI into the medical center. Declining statistics were her focus of attention. *People must not be doing their job* was her assumption. She had a negative frame. Her questions arose from that frame. They were depreciative in nature, leading to critical conversations. By reframing her focus to *possibilities for great care*, she automatically found herself asking different questions. She became curious about what was already working and about creative

Table 3.2 Examples of Generative Questions

What Your Question Can Do	Examples
Elicit information, stories, ideas, and perspectives	Alisha's question to the staff: When are patients satisfied?
Tap experience	You've done something like this before. What was your experience? What worked well for you?
Allow strengths to show up	How might each of you contribute to the success of this venture?
Surface best practices and elements of success	What best practices in the industry are you familiar with?
Move toward solutions or to information and data that inform possible solutions	Jerry's wonderment: What are mothers of healthier children doing?
Identify new ways of thinking, new possibilities, opportunities, and aspirations	As you think about thriving digital communities, what do they have that we need if we are to develop a thriving digital economy?
Inform what you might do, the results you might want	Monica's question: What can we do that allows you the car and me my sense of peace?
Make room for new knowledge, creativity, and innovation	Forget completely about how we have done this in the past. If you were designing it today, what would you do?
Deepen connections	How do you see it? What's important to you about this project?
Strengthen relationships	Can you say more about what you mean when you say there's no opportunity for you here? What are possible opportunities you are seeking?
Engage those on the sidelines	What do you think, Elizabeth?
Generate understanding	Can you say more about what you are thinking? Help me understand your perspective.

ideas for managing challenges. Her change in focus of attention ignited generative questions.

As you begin playing with positive framing and generative questions, ask yourself: Does what I am about to say add value? Am I fueling productive and meaningful engagement? Am I initiating an appreciative tone, and do my questions move us in a positive direction? Table 3.2 provides plenty of examples.

Our framing and questions are fateful. They influence our conversations. And those conversations affect both our well-being and our potential to thrive. Conversations fueled by positivity and generativity ignite individual and collective energy. They broaden and build our capacity to innovate and to act together with others for desired outcomes. Try positive framing and asking generative questions wherever you can. Pay attention to the outcomes. You will see that these two practices facilitate effective and efficient change for you and others in your family, organization, and communities.

In the next chapter, we'll share five rules for using these two practices most effectively. As we will show, the five AI principles helped Daniel, Ravi, and several other clients expand their ability to engage in conversations that were definitely worth having.

4

What's Driving Your Conversation?

> *Each person's life is lived as a series of conversations.*
> *— Deborah Tannen*

Tone and direction are simple cues that tell us what kind of conversation we are in. How we got into that kind of a conversation is a different story, yet it is an important one to understand if we want to make sure we have conversations that feel good (on balance) and that take us where we want to go. If we are not aware of what's driving our conversations, it is much more difficult to practice positive framing and generative questions. Our personal frame, expectations, and assumptions can get in the way. Fortunately, David Cooperrider has identified a set of explicit principles—the Appreciative Inquiry Principles—that underlie your success with the two practices. These principles can guide your awareness, putting you in the driver's seat and strengthening your capacity for engaging in conversations worth having.

During Alisha's AI training, she learned that human interactions rest on a set of five rules, or principles.[1] Recall from chapter 1 her reaction: She realized she was part of the problem. She became aware of her own frame and assumptions and of how they were influencing her conversations. That awareness changed everything for her. It was essential to her success in applying the two practices. The five principles enable us to understand what's driving the tone and direction of any conversation. Whether it be appreciative or depreciative, these principles are in effect. The five AI principles are as follows:

1. Constructionist Principle: Understanding, interpersonal dynamics, and ultimately our social reality are created through language and in conversation.

→ What we believe to be true is informed by and evolves through conversation.

2. Simultaneity Principle: Change happens the moment a question is asked or a statement is made.

→ As words are spoken, our mind, body, and emotions react in a split second.

3. Poetic Principle: Every person, organization, or situation can be seen and understood from many perspectives.

→ There is no one truth about any person, situation, or organization; truth depends on perception and focus of attention.

4. Anticipatory Principle: The images and thoughts we hold influence our conversation and affect our future.

→ Whatever we are anticipating, we are likely to encounter. Our expectations inform what we look for, what we see, and what we hear.

5. Positive Principle: The more positive and generative the question, the more positive and long-lasting the outcome.

→ Our questions inspire images, and imagery compels action.

The five AI principles are simple rules that govern our conversations.[2] Understanding how these principles work together can put us in the driver's seat when it comes to initiating productive and meaningful engagement. Here's how:

- If the way we talk together influences understanding, interpersonal dynamics, and teams, departments, and organizations (Constructionist Principle), then it makes sense to hold our beliefs lightly and to ask questions and make room for both new knowledge and new meaning.
- If our perceptions and experience change instantaneously in response to how we use or interpret words and actions (Simultaneity Principle), then it makes sense to stay open and ask questions.
- If our beliefs and the stories we make up about people and situations influence how we understand and how we act (Poetic Principle), then it makes sense to talk about and pay attention to what's working, what's best, and what's possible.
- If our expectations influence what we see, hear, and do (Anticipatory Principle), then it makes sense to stay open, anticipate the best from others, and expect to be pleasantly surprised.
- If our words and the questions we ask have tone and direction that engender imagery (Positive Principle), then it makes sense to ask the most generative and inspiring questions we can, and to stimulate positive images of what we want more of.

When Alisha learned about these principles, she reflected back over her previous interactions with medical center staff. She realized that her beliefs that her job was on the line and the staff was not doing *their* jobs drove those conversations. Alisha felt it was her responsibility to make sure the quarterly reports improved, yet she couldn't do that because she thought people weren't doing quality work.

She now found herself questioning whether any of that was really true. She understood that her critical questions flowed from her thoughts and feelings. In reflecting, she realized that her fear of failure made her look for someone to blame. Those conversations left everyone feeling bad. On top of that, the conversations weren't producing the results she needed. Patient satisfaction and employee engagement kept slipping. Using the AI principles, however, Alisha was able to turn around her thinking and her conversations.

Most of the time, we are not paying any attention to what is shaping our conversations. Instead, we are in the moment, without being aware of what is actually driving the conversation. Until she reflected on her conversations with the staff and nurse managers, Alisha didn't realize how critical and destructive her interactions had been. Following the principles allowed her to shift her thinking and behavior and, ultimately, the outcomes. The rules encouraged her to reflect before acting. By reflecting on the situation, she was able to see how she was making sense of it and how her sense-making was influencing both her perceptions and her actions. This reflection made her more open.

She was also able to challenge her own thinking and how she was seeing things. Becoming aware gave her the power to choose a frame that made way for a more worthwhile conversation. From this place of awareness, she could choose to be in the driver's seat. Alisha's entire approach shifted once she realized how important her frame of mind, assumptions, openness, expectations, and words were to the outcome of her conversations.

At her training, Alisha learned that the heart of AI consists of the *cooperative search for the best in people, their organizations, and the world around them* and that solving tough problems from that perspective results in creative solutions, which is *life-giving* for people.[3] When she returned to work after the training, she thought carefully about her approach and her relationships with the people with whom she interacted. In this reflective mindset, she knew the staff cared about patients even more than she did. And, of course, they wanted the medical center to be a great place to work. She still had to talk with them about the poor quarterly reports for their unit. However, this time she intended to have a conversation that was productive as well as meaningful.

Following the Constructionist Principle and the Poetic Principle, Alisha framed her conversation by acknowledging and affirming the staff: "I know we are understaffed and that each of you is working extra hard to make sure patients are well cared for. I have no doubt you want your diligent work and care to be reflected in our reports as much as I do." This created an appreciative context, influencing expectations (the Anticipatory Principle). Then, following the Positive Principle, she asked a generative question that stimulated a conversation worth having: "Let's forget about the reports for a minute. Tell me where you feel you are excelling in each of these areas on your floor."

At first, the staff seemed stunned at the turnabout in the tone and direction of Alisha's question. They couldn't believe that she was setting aside the reports. After a moment of awkward silence, though, the staff began sharing stories of patients who'd been fully satisfied, even to the point of sending thank-you notes and flowers to staff after they had left. Alisha asked them to be more specific about what was unique about those patients' experiences. The ensuing conversation surfaced positive actions that could be replicated.

This reflected the Simultaneity Principle and the Positive Principle in action. Some staff had never even thought of a few of the ideas. Alisha felt delighted with the increased energy and enthusiasm the staff seemed to have for one another and the patients. It was a great conversation and the beginning of the turnaround in performance and ratings. This micro-moment created a macro-movement for positive change at the medical center.

The easiest way to move in a positive direction while uplifting and energizing people is to initiate conversations worth having. To do this, it's important to understand and pay attention to what's driving our conversations. Let's explore more deeply how the AI principles can help you create great conversations. The idea is to be able to reflect on your own frame, motivations, and expectations the way Alisha did, so that you can more intentionally engage in conversations worth having. Each of the stories we share starts with a core principle, yet all the principles are at work in every conversation. These principles invite us to learn how we can drive our conversations in a positive direction in all aspects of our lives. The first principle, the Constructionist Principle, is foundational to all the rest.

The Way We Know Is Fateful

> ***Constructionist Principle:*** *Understanding, interpersonal dynamics, and ultimately reality are created through language and conversation.*[4]

At the end of the first month of school, Jamal's favorite class was social studies and his favorite teacher was Ms. Wittit. He had turned in every assignment, volunteered for extra credit, and even stayed after to help tutor one of the other kids who was struggling. He was thriving. While in the teacher's lounge one day, Ms. Wittit shared how excited she was to have Jamal in her classroom and bragged about what a great student he was and how much he contributed to his classmates. Ms. Summers, who had Jamal in her English class, was dumbfounded. She wondered if there could be two Jamals in the seventh grade. She shrugged her shoulders and concluded that he must not like English.

Others might come to the same conclusion, and they would be wrong. Jamal's participation and performance stemmed from classroom interactions, not his subject preference. The frame or mindset each teacher held influenced their understanding of Jamal, what they believed would support his learning, and ultimately the way they engaged with him. Let's take a look at the unexamined framing that each of these teachers brought to their classroom and the influence that framing had on Jamal.

Ms. Summers grew up in a strict household. Her mom was a nurse, and her dad was in the military. She was raised to believe that success came from disciplined action and attention to what was important. If you had a problem, you dealt with it promptly. Sometimes this meant asking for help, but doing it yourself showed character. Her mother was loving and nurturing. Her dad rarely praised her for good work, because that was expected: You work hard, you do your duty, and maybe there is time for play. She believed she could best help students learn by ensuring that they stayed focused on the class material and did good work. This was her frame in working with all her students.

Ms. Wittit grew up in a very different kind of household. Her mother was a naturopathic physician, and her dad was a successful sculptor. Their home was full of laughter, encouragement, and creativity. She was raised to believe that when you were most engaged and passionate about something, you would be successful. If you had problems, you stepped back to see the bigger picture and sought other people's perspectives and support. Her mom was loving and nurtured her strengths. Her dad inspired her to see the world through the eyes of an artist, always looking for possibilities and unique perspectives. Ms. Wittit believed she could best help students by encouraging their passion and engagement with the material and reinforcing their strengths. This was her frame in working with students.

Both teachers wanted the best for Jamal, yet their way of understanding his behavior, based on their personal frames, made a remarkable difference in how they interacted with him. In English class, Ms. Summers was trying to be helpful, though Jamal felt constantly criticized. When he tried to connect with others by making a joke, Ms. Summers admonished him immediately. He often gazed out the window to help him concentrate. Ms. Summers assumed that he was distracted, so she would stand between him and the window, hoping that would help him pay attention. Jamal's assignments were erratic. When they were done poorly or off topic, she asked, in a critical tone, "Why did you turn in such poor work when you are clearly capable of better work?" Jamal would look at his feet and shrug his shoulders. He didn't like English class much.

Ms. Wittit's interactions with Jamal were remarkably different. She believed humor could help students learn, and she saw Jamal's clowning around as a way for him to break tension, make a point, and connect with the other students. Left alone, he was careful to be appropriate and stop himself most of the time. If she needed to redirect, she was careful not to single him out or embarrass him. She noticed Jamal gazed out the window a lot, and she wondered if he might be a highly auditory learner. She knew that auditory learners often look away in order to concentrate. She tested her theory by occasionally asking him a question about what she'd been saying. He'd turn toward her and answer correctly and promptly each time. Clearly, he was paying attention, so she ignored his window-gazing behavior.

The first time he did poorly on a homework assignment, she stopped him after class and said, "Jamal, you are an excellent student. Your first three papers were spot on and written well. What you turned in yesterday doesn't really reflect the assignment. Is there a reason you didn't write on topic?" Jamal told her that he wasn't really sure what she'd said when she assigned it and was too embarrassed to ask. None of his friends were in this class, and he didn't have anyone to ask, so he'd guessed.

She exclaimed, "Oh my, we have to change that! If you don't understand what the assignment is, imagine how many others might not understand it either. I really need you to

---

Table 4.1 Principles at Work in Jamal's Story

Constructionist Principle

Ms. Summers
Worldview: A meaningful and successful life comes from following rules, using disciplined action, and solving problems quickly. Therefore, talk about and follow rules, enforce discipline promptly, and problem-solve in order to be successful.

Ms. Wittit
Worldview: A meaningful and successful life comes from following your passions and heart, acting from strengths, and using creative thinking to inspire possibility. Therefore, talk about and inspire passion, discover strengths, and make room for creative potential.

Poetic Principle

Ms. Summers
She sees Jamal as a potentially bright student who has some behavior issues that get in the way of his success. She thinks about how to curtail his weaknesses to create a successful learning environment.

Ms. Wittit
She sees Jamal as bright with acute hearing and wonders if his shyness may be getting in the way of his success. She thinks about how to leverage his strengths to create a successful learning environment.

Simultaneity Principle

Ms. Summers
The moment Jamal starts clowning, she quickly stops it so he can learn. Jamal feels shamed and shuts down in response to her public reprimands and her criticism of the assignment. He is afraid to answer her questions.

Ms. Wittit
The moment Jamal gazes out the window, she asks a question to assess his attention. Jamal feels seen and encouraged in response to her questions in class, and he is encouraged to be honest with her in response to what he sees as genuine curiosity about his assignment.

Anticipatory Principle

Ms. Summers
If she can spot his behavioral problems when they show up and quickly stop them, Jamal might be more successful. She expects there will be behavioral issues, and she is on the lookout for them. Jamal is afraid to answer her questions because he expects further criticism, which he's heard before: "Well, don't be so silly. Speak up and ask me!"

Ms. Wittit
If she looks for ways to engage him and help him use his strengths, he'll be more successful. She anticipates he has strengths and interests, and she's looking for them. Jamal has been supported and encouraged in the classroom, so he expects the same thing when she asks about the assignment.

Positive Principle

Ms. Summers
The questions that are asked are critical in nature, designed to help him improve.

Ms. Wittit
The questions that are asked are appreciative in nature, designed to surface information and encourage Jamal.

---

make sure I'm clear. What could you say or do to let me know I need to repeat something more clearly the next time?" Jamal thought for a moment and joked, "I could scratch my head and make a silly face?" He demonstrated, and they both laughed. He agreed he'd try that the next time he didn't quite get the assignment. After that, Jamal never hesitated to use the signal to repeat something he thought was important. He was making straight A's, and he loved social studies. Table 4.1 provides a summary comparison of the principles, working from two different frames.

This is the Constructionist Principle in action. In any given moment, each of us brings to it a wealth of knowledge and experience, plus our personal frame and a set of beliefs that shape and influence our perception. All of these elements influence how we respond to the present moment. First, we "construct" understanding about the way the world works. Then those mental models govern our perceptions, understanding, and subsequent actions. Ms. Summers and Ms. Wittit each developed a unique worldview as they grew up having conversations with their family, friends, teachers, and other influential people. Their worldview governed how they understood Jamal and the meaning they made of his actions. This influenced their interactions with him. Unless we stop, reflect, and become aware that our hidden frame is driving our conversation, we end up reinforcing our own frame and possibly eclipsing others. This simple awareness means that we have the option to choose to be open, challenge our own perception, ask generative questions, and entertain a *new* frame.

Change Happens the Moment You Ask the Question

> **Simultaneity Principle:** *Change happens the moment a question is asked or a statement is made.*

Recall in the last chapter how Gabriela suddenly became aware of the tone and direction of the conversation she was having with the provost. That awareness allowed her to check her negative actions and ask a generative question. Gabriela felt in awe of how quickly the provost's behavior changed and how fast the conversation flipped. In that instant, she understood the power of the Simultaneity Principle: Inquiry and change are *not* separate moments.

Her story illustrates how easy it can be to turn a conversation around with a simple generative question. It shows that *change begins the moment you ask a question or make a comment.* To experience this yourself, think of the last time you made a mistake in front of your boss or colleagues or were chastised publicly. Stop reading for a moment and bring the memory in and feel the experience in your body. How does reliving that experience affect you physically, emotionally, and mentally? Now, recall the last time you were praised publicly or were acknowledged at work for excellence. Stop for a moment again and bring that memory in. How does reliving that affect you physically, emotionally, and mentally?

How fast did your state change? You probably found that it was simultaneous with the suggestion. That shows the Simultaneity Principle. Inquiry and change, for all intents and purposes, are simultaneous events in a conversation. Gabriela's question to the provost shifted his body, tone, and direction instantaneously. She also discovered there were (at least) two stories about the faculty and the project. In one story, faculty are resistant to technology. In the other, faculty are embracing it. Which story turns up in a conversation depends on the frame you are using and the questions you ask (the Poetic Principle). Next, we'll see how Daniel learns the power of the Poetic Principle in his work with First Nation's gang members.

The Story in Front of Us Influences Our Expectations

> *Poetic Principle: Every person, organization, or situation can be seen and understood from many perspectives.*

Daniel worked with First Nation's youth and had an especially challenging job of trying to help gang members choose a different path. He had been taking these troubled groups on ropes course adventures to teach them teamwork and leadership skills,[5] though without much success. Daniel did not believe these gang members knew much about teamwork or leadership, as evidenced both by their failure to complete challenges and by the life

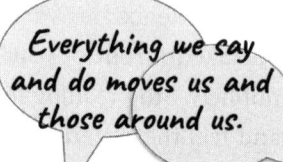

Everything we say and do moves us and those around us.

choices they were making. He had hoped that if he could teach them these skills, they might take a leadership role in their own lives.

One day a grant came through for him to purchase a portable challenge course, which included training. During his training, he was introduced to a different kind of facilitation: Appreciative Facilitation.[6] Instead of pointing out why teams failed at activities, this process invited participants to identify moments of success and build on strengths. During the training, Daniel was introduced to the AI principles, and he had a major "aha!" moment, just like Alisha. He reflected on the assumptions and stories he believed about the gang members and understood how they were influencing the way he saw them, what he listened for, and what he said to them. Without knowing it, he had been reinforcing his beliefs in their incompetence, and he felt dismayed that his debriefing style had actually reinforced their negative behaviors.

When he started facilitating with generative questions, a whole different story began to emerge. One of his first questions was simple: "Even though you didn't complete the challenge, what was working for you?" As they struggled with this shift in focus, Daniel tried to remember witnessing something that was working so that he could cue them.

"Remember when you were able to stay on the beams and began to move the team across the swamp? What did you do to help you to stay on the beam and move as a team?" One young man volunteered, "We were holding on to each other. That helped us balance." Then more of them voiced ideas: "We moved slowly, and we didn't pull someone until they were ready." "Sammy wasn't on yet, and he could tell us what was happening because he could see everybody. That helped me focus."

In that moment, Daniel realized these kids actually *had* teamwork and leadership skills. They used them to be a tight gang. He just hadn't looked for them. Over time, his questions surfaced skills in each young man, and some of them discovered they were strong leaders. He now saw his job as helping them realize how capable they were and cultivating their strengths to be effective leaders in the community. Over the next year, Daniel's struggle turned into joy as he watched the potential of these kids emerge. He inspired them to create new challenge activities using the modular equipment, and he taught them appreciative facilitation so that they could teach younger boys what they had learned.

Daniel experienced the Poetic Principle. When he was watching for failures, he saw failure. When he was looking for teamwork and leadership, he saw leadership and team competence. It was neither magic nor Pollyannaish. It was simply a matter of choosing a positive perspective and then asking generative questions.[7] The next story builds on this principle, as Ravi discovers that creating a positive frame for a conversation and asking a generative question are not enough to ensure that you'll have a conversation worth having.

Expectations Influence Conversations and Possibilities

Anticipatory Principle: We move in the direction of the images and thoughts we hold.

On his first effort to practice positive framing and generative questions with his team, Ravi discovered the importance of the Anticipatory Principle. Ravi was a senior leader in a large international technology organization headquartered in India. The company operated with a top-down leadership model. In an effort to compete with smaller high-tech startups, the company had invested in AI leadership development with the goal of increasing agility, innovation, and engagement.

Hold your viewpoint lightly. Make room for new perspectives.

Ravi had attended the workshops and saw the value of AI. He wanted his team to be more engaged and feel ownership of the business. He decided to involve them in his project design before he turned the final draft over to the vice president. He had already worked on the design for several months. Now it was all but finalized, and he felt comfortable sharing it. He presented it to his team and asked what he thought was a generative question: "I would like to hear what you have to say about this proposed project before I submit it. What questions or suggestions do you have?"

The team, pleased to be asked, did ask questions and make suggestions, some of which challenged the basic strategy and structure of his plan. Ravi got defensive and began advocating for the plan, explaining why his design was the right one. After a while the team stopped engaging. One of the members whispered to a colleague, "Why did he ask us if he wasn't open to our suggestions? What a waste of time!"

The meeting ended, and Ravi felt that he'd completely failed to implement the AI practices. What had happened? The answer was not in Ravi's questions; it was in what lay behind the questions. Ravi had put in months' worth of work on a design he thought was final. He was anticipating that he would simply get approval from the team, and they would feel good about being asked. The whispering team member identified the issue: A genuinely generative question can only be extended if we are open to hearing and welcoming responses, even those that challenge us.

Had Ravi been open to their responses, he might have asked more questions that could have teased out their thinking and ideas, which could have resulted in changing the design or reinforcing the design he had crafted. For example, Ravi might have responded to the team's questions about his strategy by saying, "Tell me more about your ideas. What do you like most about my proposal and what suggestions do you have to make it even better?" The responses might have shed light on ideas he hadn't considered, or it might have helped his team learn new information that further strengthened his strategy.

Ravi's situation is not uncommon. When we have invested a lot in something we've created or we deeply believe in, we tend to advocate for it. For this reason, it pays to invite engagement up front in the early stages. Imagine how Ravi might have reacted had he brought his initial thinking to the team after only one week, with the same positive frame and generative questions. Uncommitted to his own outcome and expecting creative ideas, he would have been open to valuable input. This would have generated a very different conversation, most likely one worth having.

Ravi's story illustrates how images and thoughts influence the tone and direction of our conversations. His story began with his belief that his team would approve his plan, and this belief blocked his ability to be open to authentic responses to his questions. Ravi's experience was not unique. In our work with clients, we've discovered that most of us are constantly planning, anticipating, musing, worrying, imagining, thinking, wondering, and assuming. This seemingly passive activity affects our expectations. Those expectations influence the way we see, listen, and talk. So taking the time to reflect on our own thinking and expectations helps us stay open to possibilities.

In our last story, Jack also has positive expectations, and he discovers the power of using a positive question to unlock meaningful moments with his children.

Positive Question, Positive Outcome

Positive Principle: The more positive and generative our questions, the more positive and long-lasting the outcomes.

Jack's story is an all-too-common one among those who have children. Many parents have struggled to engage their children in a conversation about their day by asking the simple, open-ended question "How was school today?" Jack was no different, until he followed the positive principle. Jack was a manager in a manufacturing plant who happened to share a more personal story with us. One day he confided, "I do my best to be home in time to tuck

What is the best thing that happened today?

my three children in to bed each night. I used to ask them how their day went and if anything happened at school that day. I would always get the same answers: *good* and *nothing.*" He shrugged, "How could a child be in school all day and say that nothing happened?" Then he smiled. "One evening, I asked my oldest son, who is eight, a more positive question: 'What was the best thing that happened at school today?'"

"What?" his son replied, alerted by a different question. Jack asked it again. His son thought about it for a moment. His face lit up. He told his dad about how they got to dissect a snake and how cool it was. He also shared that their class earned a special pizza lunch because they had earned the most reading points.

Jack anticipated that his children had school stories to share, but he had not been able to surface them. Much to his delight, his positive question changed the tone and direction of his conversations with his children. He learned a lot from this first conversation. He discovered new ways to engage his kids. This eventually led him to try such questions at the plant with his employees, where it was equally successful.

The Positive Principle, sometimes referred to as the Generative Principle, is the idea that the more positive our questions and comments, the more positive our actions and potential. Bold, generative questions, like Jack's, inspire strong, affirmative images. Research shows that we naturally move in the direction of the images that are stimulated by such questions.[8] All the more reason to make them as generative as possible. If we look at each of the stories in this chapter, conversations worth having ultimately depended on the way the person framed or understood the situation and the questions each person asked:

Table 4.2 Appreciative Inquiry Principles Summary

Principle	Essence of the Principle
Constructionist Principle	• We jointly construct our social realities through our shared conversations, and then our social reality influences the way we talk. • When we change the way we talk together, the questions we ask, and so on, we change the present reality. • *Words create worlds.*
Simultaneity Principle	• Change happens the moment we ask the question, or the moment we make a comment or enter the conversation. • *Inquiry is intervention.*
Poetic Principle	• There are many perspectives, multiple ways of knowing and understanding. How we understand a situation or a person and what story we tell about it affects everything. • *You have a choice in how you see things.*
Anticipatory Principle	• We move in the direction of our thoughts and the images that we hold. • What we focus on expands. • *We see what we expect to see; what we look for, we find.*
Positive (Generative) Principle	• The questions we ask and what we inquire into are generative. The more positive and generative the questions, the more positive and generative the outcome. • *Positive images and positive actions produce positive results.*

Note: For more information on the five classic principles of Appreciative Inquiry, see the AI Commons, available at https://appreciativeinquiry.champlain.edu/learn/appreciative-inquiry-introduction/5-classic-principles-ai/.

- Alisha: "Tell me, where are you excelling in each of these areas on your floor?"
- Ms. Wittet: "What are his strengths? When is he most engaged and excited about learning?"
- Ms. Wittet: "What could you say or do to let me know I need to repeat something more clearly the next time?"
- Gabriela: "Are there any faculty who are on board with what you are trying to do?"
- Daniel: "Remember when you were able to stay on the beams and began to move the team across the swamp? That was exciting! What did you do to stay on the beams and move as a team?"
- Jack: "What was the best thing that happened at school today?"

The five principles are summarized in Table 4.2.

Everything that we say and do moves us and those around us. Our tone and direction, governed by these five principles, influence those conversations. The next time you find yourself in a conversation, take a moment to reflect on what's driving that conversation. Are you coming from an appreciative or depreciative frame? What are your expectations? Are you willing to challenge your assumptions, to stay open and curious long enough to be surprised and delighted at what you might discover? If you are, then you're on track to be the driver of conversations worth having.

In the next chapter, we'll explore how to formally use the two practices and five principles to fuel productive and meaningful engagement for both organizational and community change. At the systems level, you can use a formal AI methodology called the 5-D Cycle to initiate worthwhile conversations around important and consequential topics.

5

Scaling Up Great Conversations

> *A leader is best when people barely know he exists. When his work is done, his aim fulfilled, they will say: We did it ourselves.*
>
> *– Lao Tzu*

When you think about people having productive and worthwhile conversations, how many individuals do you assume are in the conversation? You probably know intuitively what the research tells us: If there are more than eight to twelve people, you can't really have a meaningful conversation. We know that conversations worth having energize and motivate people. We also know they are productive and meaningful. Imagine the potential for organizations and communities if we could have those kinds of conversations with the whole system!

This potential has, in fact, already been achieved in cities such as Cleveland and Denver and in countries as different as Nepal and Chile. Contrary to what research would have us believe, these powerful whole-systems conversations have taken place with 50, 100, even 4,500 people at the same time. It has also happened in thousands of organizations around the world, including Google, Accenture, Verizon, ANZ Bank of Australia, Green Mountain Coffee Roasters, Nutrimental, Bibb County Schools (Georgia), Clarke Group, the U.S. Navy, the Cleveland Clinic, World Vision, the United Way of America, and the United Nations Global Compact.[1] One of our favorite organizations is Fairmount Santrol, which has been using Appreciative Inquiry (AI) to engage people in worthwhile, whole-system conversations for over fifteen years.[2] Jenniffer Deckard, its CEO, recently shared the following:

> *We are a flourishing enterprise because of AI. AI is contagious and its principles have so much meaning to our employees. We put it into practice in our meetings, strategy sessions, annual reports, new innovations, and culture. AI applies everywhere and anywhere from our families to our working together to solve complex issues.*[3]

It may be hard to imagine having a great conversation at the system level. Yet it is actually made possible because the AI practices are formalized in a structured process that catalyzes whole-system conversations worth having. The process is called the Appreciative Inquiry 5-D Cycle, named for its five phases: *Define, Discover, Dream, Design,* and *Deploy.* Let's take a look at what happened when this process was used to catalyze a new venture abroad.

Gerard Krupp was president of a German automotive sup-
plier. The company was faced with mounting challenges from
its original equipment manufacturers (OEMs) and suppliers
in the United States. In addition, it needed a clearer direction,
stronger customer relationships, and improved profitability.
The solution was to set up a second Technology Center in
Michigan to be closer to the automotive OEMs. Gerard was
sure that this was the way to meet the multiple demands from
his customers. However, he knew that it wouldn't be easy. He
had a team of talented, committed, hardworking people who
stuck their necks out for him time after time. Asking members
of the Technology Center in Germany to pick up their families
and move to the United States was going to be a bold move.

For two reasons, Gerard chose Erich to be the program
manager to lead the move. Erich had the ability to work across
silos. This capability was important because the Technology
Center's administration, technology, sales and marketing, and
R&D teams did not currently collaborate well. Erich was going
to have to hire several additional U.S. employees and create
a unified team as well as a winning strategy to drive growth.
Over the past seven years in Germany, Erich had demonstrated
his ability to lead conflicting teams in meaningful dialogues
that resulted in win-win outcomes.

For the first thirty days in the new location, the trans-
planted teams set up shop while anticipating that headquarters would send a game plan for them. As people typically
do, those who moved took their current office culture with
them. They reproduced the workplace customs and climate
they knew, thus being loyal to their functional team. But it
was a challenge for the newly hired American employees to
find their place in that climate. In general, no one thought to
share information or planning outside their own small team.

Conversations across those divides were infrequent. When they did occur, they were often critical and destructive.

Meanwhile, Erich knew that he could not wait for corporate to tell them what to do and how to do it. Having attended an AI professional development workshop a few years earlier, Erich planned to unite the separate teams into one that worked collaboratively. He wanted them to focus collectively on increasing existing business and driving new business for the whole organization. He planned to accomplish this by changing the tone and direction of the conversations among team members. To initiate that, he engaged all of them in a center-wide conversation to design a strategic plan using the 5-D Cycle.

Erich knew that the 5-D Cycle would leverage the team's knowledge and experience to create unprecedented change. This more-formal methodology for using positive framing and generative questions promised to unite the Tech Center, eliminate silos, and generate a shared vision and plan for achieving the center's purpose. Since the framing for a systems conversation is just as important as it is for a one-on-one interaction or a meeting, Erich knew it would be important to have the perspectives from each of the different areas as well as both countries involved in creating that frame. So he brought together a representative from each area to form a six-person core team. To enlist them in planning the event, the first thing he did was to explain AI and the 5-D Cycle.[4]

Overview of the 5-D Cycle

Erich began his first meeting with the core team by saying, "Most of us want to continue to create a company that excels, to feel inspired at work, and to make meaningful contributions. What if we all felt free to innovate and create new possibilities for products, services, and processes that will help

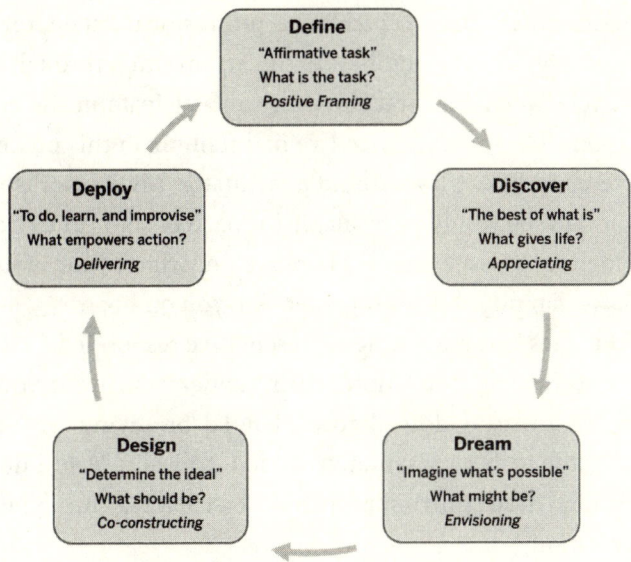

Figure 5.1 Appreciative Inquiry 5-D Cycle

shape a bold future for our organization? If I could show you an idea for how we might get to that future, would you join me in making it happen?"

He went on to tell them about his experience with AI. He shared a few stories about how other companies were using it. His core team seemed enthusiastic and curious about how they could proceed. Erich then showed them the 5 Ds (see Figure 5.1) and explained what each of the *D*s stood for. He explained, "At each phase of the cycle, we'll have worthwhile conversations that will generate meaningful information and creative possibilities for our team and our work together. Those conversations will enable us to identify our strengths and values and to create positive images of our shared future. We will also design pathways to achieve that future and collectively decide how to put those solutions into practice."

Erich noted that, typically, a professional facilitator is engaged to guide the members of the organization through the 5-D Cycle, freeing all stakeholders to participate in the conversations. He added, "Since I've had training in this process, I'd like us to give it try without a facilitator. My AI workshop trainer said she would be available to coach or support us from the sidelines. We are small. There are only thirty-four of us. I think we can pull this off together. Are you on board?"

The sales and marketing representative responded, "I love your enthusiasm, but I don't really understand what you're asking us to do. I don't know what I'd be saying 'yes' to." Martha, the tech representative, added cynically, "And I don't understand how thirty-four people can have a 'meaningful conversation.'"

"Great questions!" replied Erich. "First, most of the conversations are among small groups, like six to eight people. Larger group conversation happens when small groups share and merge their ideas. Using this 5-D Cycle will be pretty straightforward for what we are trying to do." Then he went on to explain briefly what the 5 Ds were and how the cycle flowed:

1. In **D**efine, this core planning team will use *positive framing* to clarify the task or focus for our inquiry and to create generative questions that we will ask in the Discover phase.
2. In **D**iscover, we'll engage in one-on-one interviews and small group discussions, based on the questions we crafted in the Define phase. The purpose of this phase is to identify our strengths, which is the *positive core* of our system, along with our purpose and possibilities for the future.
3. In **D**ream, we'll create shared images of the future, present them in creative and imaginative ways, and write vision statements.

4. In **D**esign, we'll develop prototypes for ways to move toward our vision, leveraging our positive core and staying focused on our mission.

5. In **D**eploy, we'll further develop our prototype(s) and adopt a learner mindset. This will help us evolve toward our desired future. We will learn and adapt as we move forward by continuously engaging in worthwhile conversations.

Erich asked if there were any questions. Joep, the sales rep, asked, "Who will participate in these conversations?" Erich replied, "What if all thirty-four participated in the same set of conversations at the same time? If we want to be one united team, then we had better be one team when we discover our strengths, create a vision, and plan our future, don't you think? Are you in?" Erich got thumbs up from each representative. The adventure was about to begin!

Define Phase: Framing the Task and Crafting Generative Questions

Erich had closed the first meeting by asking the core team members to think about why using this approach would be valuable for them. At their next team meeting, Erich opened by asking them, "If you had a chance to think about why this approach would be good to use, what did you come up with?" Each representative had different responses. Erich heard things like:

- *I like the idea of inspiring us to work together and owning this center as a whole team.*
- *I went back and shared what we talked about with my team, and they really liked the idea of being included in creating our vision and plan. They're excited!*

- *I think this could make a difference in how we work and the positive impact we could have. It's about time we showed everyone our positive side and our strengths!*

Heads were nodding around the table as team members spoke. Erich smiled. He knew how important it was for everyone to be on the same page about *why* they were using this approach. His next question to the group was "What are your highest hopes for the outcome from our conversations?" Erich captured their ideas as they spoke:

- *Unity*
- *Alignment*
- *Collaboration*
- *The kind of team that will create unheard-of growth for the company, and for our customers*
- *A shared sense of purpose, direction, and strategy*

He was delighted that they had named everything he was hoping for. Erich asked one additional question: "We know our corporate goal: growth from increased sales. What are some of the challenges or issues that we need to address in order to do that?" Again, he captured their comments:

- *No one knows exactly what our purpose is; we don't have a mission.*
- *We don't know where we're going. We don't have a vision!*
- *And there's no plan, no directive about what we're going to do and how to do it!*
- *We've never worked as one unified team; I'm not sure we know how to do that. We don't play very well together.*
- *We don't really know one another's strengths, much less appreciate them.*

It was clear to everyone that they needed purpose and direction. Erich framed their next conversation this way: "We know what headquarters wants: Help grow the company by increasing sales to current and new customers. That's all we really need to know from them. If there's anything I've learned in life, it's that people commit to what they help create. Let's not wait for instructions from headquarters—let's create our own mission, vision, and strategic plan!" This lit a fire under the core team. "Where do we start?" the R&D representative asked.

"We start by creating a positive frame," he replied. "This means clarifying our task for our strategic planning meeting. It will be important for us to identify an affirmative task. That means getting really clear on what we want, or what we want more of, in order to achieve what the company wants." Erich introduced *flipping* to guide the core team through positive framing. He asked the group to identify the core issue standing in their way of achieving consistent growth. The team landed on these core issues:

- **Name It:** *As a center, we have no plan, and we don't know where we're headed, so we can't really work together well.*

The team first worked together to identify the positive opposite, and then created the positive frame or affirmative task:

- **Flip It/The Positive Opposite:** *We have a plan, we know where we're going, and we work well together.*
- **Frame It/The Affirmative Task:** *We are a high-performing center with one dynamic team, one vision, one shared mission, and a plan.*

Just seeing this frame, the core team immediately got excited about the future possibilities. Erich suggested, "In order to accomplish this together, let's make sure we figure out the positive core we bring to becoming a unified, high-performing team. We'll also need a mission and a vision we believe in, as well as a plan to deliver on our mission. What do you think? Are there other tangible outcomes we want from our meeting?" The core team agreed that those were all that were needed.

Culture and climate emerge from our conversations.

Erich explained that the next step in this phase was crafting questions that would surface positive experiences of high-performance teamwork, key employee strengths, central purpose, and values that would support the center as one team. This would clarify their positive core. They needed to craft two sets of questions. The first step was to devise questions as a guide for one-on-one interviews. Erich showed them a set of classic AI interview questions to help all of them think through the questions they needed to craft (see Table 5.1).

The core team worked a long time, putting great care into ensuring that questions were positively framed to elicit stories and conversations that would help the team discover their true potential. The questions also needed to help them learn more about the organization and think through their ultimate purpose. Their final interview guide contained these five questions:

1. Describe a high-point experience working as a team in the Technology Center or organization—a time when you felt most alive and engaged as a member of the team.

2. What is it that you value about yourself, your colleagues, and the organization?
3. When our center is at its best, what are the core factors (our strengths) that give it life, without which the center would simply not be at its best?
4. Imagine that three years from now the company has grown significantly. Describe the ways in which we work together as one team and how that has enabled the Tech Center to contribute to the organization's success. What business segment(s), technical product(s), or process innovation(s) have been successfully created and launched?
5. What three wishes do you have to strengthen our center or the organization itself?

Erich explained, "After the one-one interviews, groups of six to eight people will come together and interviewers will share the high points of their partners' stories, not their own. This will encourage people to listen for understanding and help

Table 5.1 Five Classic Questions for an Appreciative Inquiry Interview

The first three questions focus on the best of what *is*.	1. What would you describe as a high-point experience in your organization? 2. What do you value most about yourself, your work, and your organization? 3. What gives life to your organization?
The next question focuses on what *might be*, or possibilities.	4. Imagine that it's three years later, and everything you ever thought possible is happening at your organization. What's going on? How have things changed?
The final question helps transition to what *can be*.	5. What three wishes do you have to enhance the health and vitality of your organization?

build positive relationships. Our next task is to design those conversations. We need to structure them so small groups can tease out important themes and ideas from their interviews." The core team came up with the following instructions:

1. **Discover.** Share the highlights of your partner's answer to question 1 and what stood out for you from questions 2 and 3. Capture the ideas so that everyone can see them. After everyone has shared, have a conversation as a group about key themes that emerged. Identify important values and strengths.
2. **Discover.** Based on our core values and strengths, write a brief but focused mission statement.
3. **Dream.** Share your partner's vision of our Technology Center in three years. What stood out for you that was exciting or inspiring? Capture everyone's ideas so others can see them. Once everyone has shared, have a conversation about our future. Create a shared vision for the Tech Center.
4. **Dream.** What were your partner's three wishes? Capture them so that they can be shared with everyone.

After this meeting, the core team seemed very happy with how they had defined the upcoming strategic planning meeting. Erich told them that at their next meeting they would set a date and design the flow for the meeting.

When the core team regrouped the following week, Erich explained how the meeting would flow through the four remaining Ds: Discover, Dream, Design, and Deploy. Their focus for this last Define phase meeting was to design the agenda, using the remaining four phases, and also to create any further instructions for small-group conversations and planning. They followed with a logistics plan, divided up responsibilities, and left excited to generate enthusiasm among the other members of their teams.

A Look Inside Their Strategic Planning Meeting: The 4Ds

All thirty-four employees gathered for a one-day strategic planning session.[5] Erich opened by reading the following statement:

> Our company made the investment to move all of us to this office in Michigan to be near our key customers, instilling in us the charge to drive more growth for our organization.
>
> There is no guarantee that we will have business tomorrow, and it won't simply be waiting on our doorstep just because we are here now. In the past sixty days, it became clear to me that it is our opportunity and responsibility to create our future and not wait for corporate to tell us what to do.
>
> We must realize it is a privilege to be the supplier of choice, and it is our responsibility to be the best at what we do to make it happen. Today, we shall discover our center's strengths— what we do best. We will create a mission statement and guiding vision that inspire and clarify our purpose and direction. We will wrap up this session knowing what we do best, how we best work together, and what our unique value offering is. This will allow us to dive deeper into our core strengths and enable us to create opportunities and design strategic goals and objectives with a collaborative action plan for a shared, preferred future with measurable results.
>
> Today, we are part of a team that has been responsible for approximately $60 million in annual revenue. Tomorrow, let us be the team that leads this company to the top of our industry.
>
> We need to be innovative and inspire each other into action.

Let's create our future as a high-performing center—one dynamic team, one vision, one shared plan. Are you in?

Discover Phase: Appreciating What Gives Life

The meeting started with one-on-one interviews, using the questions the core team had crafted. To build relationships and knowledge across silos, the core team asked people to pair up with someone they did not know or work with regularly. Following the interviews, three interview pairs formed small groups of six. Guided by the Discover instructions (see page 96), people shared their interview partner's story and what stood out for them as key concepts and ideas related to the task. Then, each group identified common themes from their stories and drafted a mission statement. Each small group shared their themes and mission statement with the larger group. The large group sorted the themes and chose those that they believed made up their positive core for a unified team with one plan and one vision. Over lunch, a small group of people merged the ideas from the mission statements into a single shared statement.

Erich and the core team could feel the excitement in the room; the energy was palpable. People were talking across silos, learning about each other, and identifying important concepts that would grow their capacity to thrive as a Center while also contributing to organizational success. The Discover phase of their meeting surfaced the following values, strengths, and mission for moving to a state where the Center would be a unified, high-performing team:

Values: Dedication, flexibility, creativity, innovation, team spirit, and continuous communications. These values are how we will work collaboratively.

Strengths:
1. Adaptable: Being highly flexible to deal with change and challenges.
2. Dedicated to Customers: "That's why we moved here." We will continue to exceed internal and external customer expectations.
3. Strong Product Core: We can supply uniquely optimized sealants and adhesives.
4. Top-Notch Employees: Our employees are highly capable and are up to date in their fields.

Based on six core values and four strengths, the four teams converged on the following mission statement:

We are a dedicated and flexible team that designs, develops, and provides cost-effective and innovative engineering, NVH, sealant, and adhesive solutions that are manufactured to your specifications. We do this in a safe working environment where we retain top-quality employees.

The room was buzzing; people were talking about how affirming and inspiring this approach was and what great conversations they were having with people they didn't really know. Erich introduced the next activity on the agenda: the Dream Phase. He explained, "We don't need to identify weaknesses and threats, because we know them. That's why we relocated. We need to come up with a plan that has a vision to inspire each of us to support our customers' and prospective customers' needs and anticipated needs. That begins with dreaming big!"

Dream Phase: Envisioning What Might Be

Guided by the Dream instructions (see page 96), the same small groups drew on and amplified their positive core to create shared images of the future. Their conversations centered on *what might be . . . a chance to envision the organization at its best, the ideal high-performing center team, and a community where all members could flourish.* Imagining a desired future and creating literal images shifted people from abstract thinking to creative possibilities, freeing them to explore a shared vision.

The core team had designed this activity to encourage playfulness and inspiration. Small groups created skits and posters. These gave everyone a tangible, sensory understanding of new ways of working together. They also each crafted a written statement to accompany their visual. The vision statements were short, catchy, affirmative, and inspirational.

The whole room came alive with laughter, excitement, and potential during the presentations. To move toward a shared vision that represented the whole group, they did a Vision Walk, an exercise in which everyone reviewed the images and vision statements and then placed sticky dots on those vision statements with which they resonated most. During lunch, a second small group merged the high-vote visions into a single image and vision statement, and the group confirmed it:

> *To be the global leader providing best-in-class engineering, NVH, sealant, and adhesive solutions with exceptional customer service that exceeds our customers' expectations on time.*

The energy and synergy created during this phase carried participants into the Design phase after lunch. This was when they identified strategies and actions to make their vision a reality.

Design Phase: Co-Constructing What Should Be

After lunch, the group did a gallery walk to look at all that had been generated earlier. They were tasked with identifying ideas that called out to them, opportunities that triggered their passions. Then, they generated possibilities: strategies and actions for achieving their dream. People self-organized into small groups around these possibility topics. The first thing they did was clarify the possibility by writing a descriptive statement that captured the contribution this initiative would make to the company. Next, they designed a prototype. Starting with a prototype freed people to see that they didn't have to wait for permission or have to get things exactly right before they could present ideas. Instead, there in the meeting they could design and test their initial thinking. The core team had created some great questions to stimulate small-group design conversations:

- How will we make this happen easily?
- At this moment, what can we design rapidly and test with our colleagues?
- What's the story we would like to tell about how we will do this?
- If we were creating a business to do only this one thing, what would that business be, and what product or service would it provide?

A techie from one of the groups smiled and said, "This is like a *hackathon*." If she meant that this activity was to "hack" the current ways of doing and thinking in order to make room for creativity and innovation, she was right.

When it was time to share prototypes with the whole, Erich felt blown away by the creativity and knowledge base that had emerged. One team created a new sales call protocol that bridged every team, from product design to delivery. Another team created an innovative process to bring potential clients to the Technology Center to see firsthand how the firm develops custom solutions. After each presentation, Erich invited the rest of the group to provide *feedforward*—a new concept the core team was introducing: *What do you like about this prototype? What suggestions do you have to make it even better?*

The day was almost over. The outcomes from this Design phase set the stage for taking action. Implementing these prototypes and getting started on tasks were the next phases of the 5-D cycle.

Deploy Phase: Living into Empowering Action

Each group gathered for a final conversation about how to *deliver* or *deploy* their prototype. They created written plans with action steps that would move their prototype into reality. In closing, Erich reflected on the day and how excited he felt with the outcomes. He graciously thanked the planning team and explicitly drew attention to how carefully it had used positive framing and generative questions throughout its design. He spent a little time sharing these two practices with everyone, encouraging them to continue to inspire great conversations as they rolled out their plans and worked together to achieve their goals. Then he invited all those present to *tell a* brief story *about the best thing that happened today and their commitment to taking action.*

Deployment continued as people engaged in daily work following the meeting. That day inspired a whole new way of engaging in conversation. Relationships had been formed across the silos, and commitment both to one another and to their shared vision had been strengthened. The core team remained champions for the vision and mission. They made sure prototypes had the support and resources they needed to move forward.

Erich reported back to Gerard in Germany, "The conversations that took place to create the Center's mission, vision, and strategic plan went beyond my expectations. The various divisions have become boundaryless in this new tech center. I guess that's what happens when people co-create a shared purpose, vision, and plan of action. We are on fire to deliver on our plan!" Everyone was heard; everyone had a stake.

Within ninety days of launching the plan, the tech team saw improved results in productivity, sales, and communications. Morale for the new Center had risen to an all-time high, and a positive feeling of a home-away-from-the-corporate-home emerged. A team-based mentality was focusing on continuous improvement, using a results-driven mindset. The members' ability to act so successfully on the outcomes from their planning meeting was the result of their commitment to practice positive framing and generative questions as ways of being and working together.

This was the first time that any division of the company had created a strategic plan based on *all* employees' insights, and not only those of a few senior leaders. Gerard took notice of the results. He phoned Erich to ask him, "What made this relocation project a success?" Erich paused for a moment and replied, "I think it's because our strategic conversations were inclusive. Everyone mattered. Conversations centered on how we could make this a great success. People were invited to share their best selves, and the conversations unleashed the momentum to become a unified, winning team. Everyone knows that we can achieve the tasks ahead because they co-created them!"

Table 5.2 Appreciative Inquiry 5-D Cycle: Phases and Activities

5-D Cycle Phase	Activities
Phase 1: Define	1. Frame the task. 2. Craft the interview guide and small-group discussion (see Table 5.1 for generative AI questions). 3. Design how to implement Phases 2 through 5.
Phase 2: Discover	1. Engage in interviews, using the guide. 2. Share and analyze the stories in small groups, identifying the positive core, opportunities, and possibilities.
Phase 3: Dream	1. Envision the future grounded in the positive core. 2. Create shared images that ignite your sensory imagination. 3. Craft word images that align with the visual images.
Phase 4: Design	1. Generate possibilities for achieving the dream. 2. Craft possibility statements. 3. Engage in rapid prototyping.
Phase 5: Deploy	1. Craft action plans. 2. Enlist champions and commitment. 3. Take action. 4. Engage in cycles of prototyping and learning. 5. Value (not evaluate) the progress that has been made and inquire into what made it possible.

Gerard then asked, "Erich, can you teach me how to create these kinds of conversations back at corporate? We need to ignite the potential of everyone in this organization." Erich smiled and replied, "I'd be delighted. It will be easy to teach you positive framing and generative questions to help you have meaningful conversations and possibly even to guide department-size planning meetings. However, if you're talking about a whole-organization effort, I think we'll need a professional AI facilitator!"

What made this process relatively easy for Erich to use was his applied understanding of the two basic practices, his attention to the principles, his past experience with the 5-D structured approach, plus coaching from his AI trainer. Table 5.2 summarizes what Erich and his core team did for the Technology Center. You can do it with your division or department, as well. Just keep in mind what inspired Erich. He assumed that the responsibility for change resided with all the people in the Center. He realized that it is the people and their conversations that *are* the organization. They create the culture and climate in the way they talk and work together. Real organizational change begins when the people are invited to take responsibility for the system by engaging in productive, worthwhile conversations about their shared future.

Organizations and communities are socially constructed systems. People designed the structures, processes, workflows, and policies that are in place. So make sure those systems are supporting the outcomes you want. The 5-D Cycle enables people to work together to identify and amplify the *best of what is* in a system, to continuously create the *best of what can be*, and to design *how it can be*, which often means changing structures and systems. The result is that people come alive and formally commit to the future of the organization or community. Why? You'll find out in the next chapter, where you'll learn how the practice of using positive framing and generative questions affects us in ways that support our work and our lives in general.

6

It's Not Magic, It's Science!

*No matter what people tell you,
words and ideas can change the world.
– Nancy H. Kleinbaum*

If the experience of our clients, families, and colleagues detailed in the stories in this book has not convinced you that there is magic in conversations worth having, then perhaps the evidence from more than twenty-seven years of scientific research will help explain how positive framing and generative questions bring forth the best in human nature. This research falls into three distinct areas: the New Science,[1] positive image/position action, and positive psychology.[2] The net outcome of this research points to the importance of using language to inspire positive emotions, positive images, and positive actions. Science tells us to follow the 80/20 rule—a ratio of 80 percent positive emotions and imagery to 20 percent negative—to support well-being and excellence at the individual, group, and organization levels.[3] We'll begin with the New Science, which actually is not so "new" after twenty-five years.

The New Science

The New Science emerged once we had technology that allowed us to see what was happening inside the human brain and body. That technology allowed us to see what happens to our neurophysiology under different conditions. The functional magnetic resonance imaging (fMRI) enables scientists to engage people in conversations while they see which parts of the brain light up and what happens with brain chemistry under differing conditions. Neurological brain research has shown that strong beliefs and imagery actually change brain chemistry.[4] It also shows that brain chemistry influences our response to a given stimulus.

For example, Timothy, an accountant for a small accounting firm, recently had an argument with his boss that left him believing he is going to be fired. He also knows that without his income, his family can't make its mortgage. These beliefs create a neural "preset" that has him wired to react negatively when his wife suggests they go out to dinner. Had he instead had an experience with his boss that left him sure he was going to get a raise, he would have been delighted to go out to dinner with her. This knowledge opens the door for us to choose to influence our brain chemistry in order to better respond to various potentially inflammatory situations. It was for exactly this reason that the Los Angeles Police Department Drug Task Force received special training to handle drug busts.

The Task Force was about to make a drug bust. Its members were on-site, adrenaline pumping, ready for the signal to rush a building. The chief gave a hand signal, but no one moved. Instead, each officer began to breathe slowly, recalling a time when they felt deeply appreciative or grateful. They envisioned that time, recalling the imagery, the conversations, and especially the feelings. After this brief practice, the captain nodded his head and the squad then rushed the building. They broke through the door and subdued everyone present without a single shot. The arrest was a success. The situation and their beliefs about it did not change, but their pre-rush (pre-framing) practice changed their brain chemistry. The change enabled them to better respond to the tense situation they were about to encounter.

The police had practiced a technique they learned from the HeartMath Institute, a practice grounded in the institute's neurological research.[5] The institute discovered that positive imagery plus recalling positive experiences can bring the nervous system into coherence. Coherence produces brain chemistry that allows more complete access to the neocortex, which is where all reasoning and critical thinking take place. Before their training, when police prepared for a drug bust, adrenaline and images of chaos and violence created brain chemistry in them that was less coherent and highly reactive. The result was typically a more chaotic scene, one more likely to erupt with violence and even shooting and possibly deaths. In a coherent state, police officers were better able to assess the scene and to respond appropriately.

When it comes to conversations, critical or destructive ones are most often perceived as threats. A threat changes brain chemistry. It routes more oxygen and nutrition to the part of our brain responsible for keeping us safe. The greater the fear, the more oxygen is sent to support our fight-or-flight response, and the less oxygen is available for the neocortex. Having a strong sense of safety, connection, and belonging does the opposite: Oxygen and nutrients flow to all parts of the brain and nervous system, supporting high performance. Positive framing and generative questions stimulate the kind of brain chemistry that enables people to live and work at optimal capacity, which is what we desire in any relationship, organization, or community.

The HeartMath Institute's research shows that recalling experiences of appreciation and gratitude are the most effective for creating coherence.[6] When we frame a conversation positively and ask generative questions of others, we are, in effect, stimulating coherence for everyone participating in the conversation. Furthermore, if we are following the Positive Principle and asking powerful generative questions, we are also inspiring positive and bold images. So what does the research tell us about imagery?

Positive Image/Positive Action

If you found this story about the Los Angeles Drug Task Force memorable, it might be because it created an image in your mind. That's because imagery is compelling, as proven by research. We move in the direction of the images we hold.[7] Brain research shows that we process language in different parts of the brain, and it takes the whole brain for comprehension (see Figure 6.1). Imagery is processed in the right brain and abstract concepts in the left.[8] The corpus callosum, which connects the two hemispheres, enables us to understand concepts that contain both abstract words and image words.

What is striking is that imagery often trumps both intention *and* understanding. Children know what teachers mean when they say, "Don't run in the hall!" For some children, however, the "run in the hall" is overwhelmingly compelling. So they take off running, leaving a dumbfounded teacher behind. This

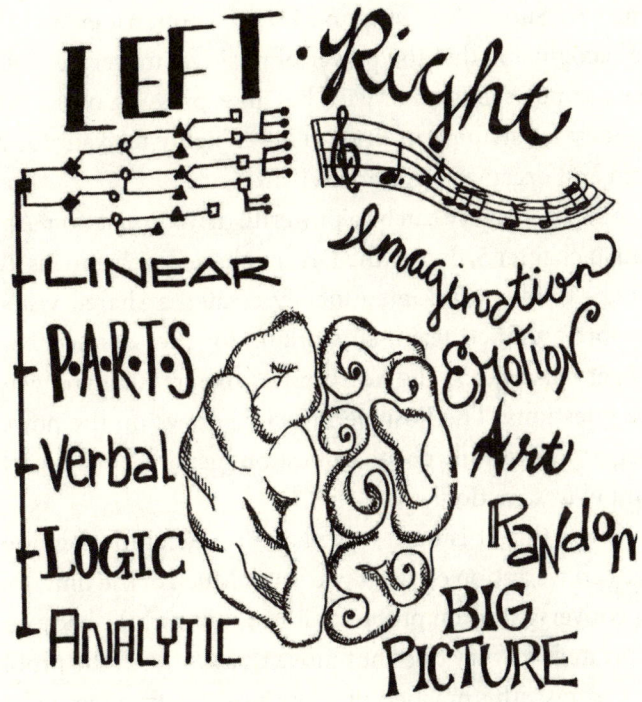

Figure 6.1 Right Brain/Left Brain Neural Processing Centers
Drawing by Caryn Brownelle Hanna, Graphic Facilitation and Illustration,
www.carynhannagraphicfacilitator.com..

is why it is more effective to tell children what you *want* them to do rather than what you *don't.* Teachers have more success when they say, *"Please walk."* That can be an equally compelling image.

The right brain doesn't know the difference between fantasy and reality; an image is just an image. Research has inspired many athletes and coaches to integrate visualization into their practice. It turns out that visualizing a perfect free throw for 50 percent of one's practice time results in higher performance than practicing the throw 100 percent of the time.[9] As Suresh Srivastva and David Cooperrider state, "We are recognizing that the power of positive imagery is not just some popular illusion or wish but an expression of the mind's capacity for shaping reality."[10] This is highly relevant for both team and organization leaders.

Shared imagery can be a powerful driver for action. As you read in chapter 5, during the Dream phase, Erich and his Technology Center team intentionally created a shared vision to support a unified team, all working for the same outcomes. Imagery also lies at the heart of positive framing and generative questions. The Positive Principle draws on the power of imagery. Powerfully positive questions generate images, which compel us to action.

Given this, it is both logical and practical to intentionally focus conversation on what you want. Much of the time, focusing conversations on problems is not worthwhile, because the associated imagery does not move us away from the problem. By contrast, the practice of using positive framing and generative questions creates images of where we want to move and what we want to achieve. Such conversations have the potential to generate powerfully positive images that compel us toward desired outcomes. *These are conversations worth having.*

It is not a new idea that positive images influence our future. Research across diverse disciplines has demonstrated that positive images generate positive action for individuals, groups, and organizations. You may be familiar with these areas of research:

- **The Placebo Effect.**[11] The belief that a pill will heal generates neurophysiological conditions in the brain and body that literally support healing. Conversations about healing an unhealthy relationship or a dysfunctional organizational climate are no different. Appreciative conversations inspire belief in the possibility of a strong and loving relationship or a climate where people thrive. Such conversations alter brain chemistry, giving us greater capacity to bring those desired futures into reality. Recall Daniel's work with the First Nations gang members. His belief about the power of positive framing and curiosity led him to ask generative questions that literally surfaced what he could not see before. What strong beliefs do *you* hold that positively influence your ability to thrive?

- **The Pygmalion Effect.**[12] The beliefs and images that we hold about others can affect the lives of those others. If the manager believes an employee can succeed, for example, the employee is much more likely to do so. The manager's belief encourages her to see the employee's potential and to provide the necessary support for his success. In addition, others see that dynamic and are influenced in how they see the employee. In turn, this influences neurophysiological coherence, giving the employee access to his full capacity to do well, even in challenging situations. Recall Jamal's experience of being in Ms. Summers' and Ms. Wittit's classes. His success or failure was directly correlated with their beliefs about him. The Pygmalion Effect and the Placebo Effect can work together to produce even greater positive results. Daniel and his young men are a case in point. His belief in the facilitation process led him to ask questions that resulted in his ability to see the strengths in the gang members. In turn, his belief in them inspired them to bring forth their leadership and teamwork ability to be successful in their activities. How are *your* beliefs about members of your family and workplace affecting their ability to thrive?

- **Positive Affect, Positive Effect.**[13] The words we use have an immediate impact on neurophysiology, our own as well as others'. The tone and direction of our conversation can influence the brain chemistry of those around us. Positive framing and generative questions influence neurophysiological coherence and make room for the full potential of individuals to come forth. This is exactly what Ms. Wittit did for Jamal. Daniel's shift to generative questions had an immediate effect on the boys. Gabriela's question to the provost caused an immediate shift in his neurophysiology, which showed up in his expression and the change in tone and direction of the conversation. See if you can have a positive impact on others' affect today, merely by asking a generative question.

The idea that positive framing is correlated with our capacity to thrive is not new. Norman Vincent Peale and Zig Zigler[14] had touted this since the 1940s and '50s. Some naysayers in recent years have dismissed their ideas as fluff. However, turn-of-the-21st-century technology has given us the ability to actually correlate neurophysiological chemistry with these ideas. Hard science now validates the value of positive framing and holding a positive attitude. The benefits for organizations and relationships are further underscored by research in the area of positive psychology.

Positive Psychology

When we engage in conversations worth having, the telltale signs are energy, creativity, and positive emotions. Research in the field of positive psychology shows that positive emotions correlate with an individual's capacity for high performance and cooperation. In the late 1990s, Barbara Fredrickson's pioneering research into the then-emerging field of positive psychology demonstrated that positive emotions literally broaden and build our capacity for higher-order thinking, creativity, empathy, cooperation, resilience, and connection.[15]

Over the last twenty years, Fredrickson's research has underscored the benefits of positivity, which is the practice of being positive or optimistic in attitude. Engaging in thoughts, behaviors, and activities that produce positive emotions actually expands our thought repertoire and increases creativity.[16] Positive emotions include more than merely joy and happiness. Fredrickson identified many emotions that generate positivity, including interest, hope, gratitude, kindness, surprise (the pleasant type), confidence, enthusiasm, satisfaction, inspiration, awe, love, and more.

Conversations that value and connect people, uncover what *is* working, and stimulate images of the ideal future that will foster many of these emotions. Fredrickson's seminal study "What Good Are Positive Emotions?" and her book that followed, *Positivity,* support that positivity creates an upward spiral of confidence and optimism.[17] This upward spiral improves health and well-being. It also expands our capacity for change, growth, learning, effective relationships, and solution-finding. This is exactly the kind of people that every organization is looking for. The good news: They are already in every organization and community. The even better news: You can bring out that best in every person, fueling productive and meaningful engagement through positive framing and generative questions.

Organization leaders will be especially interested in the research of Marcial Losada and Emily Heaphy, who studied organization teams.[18] They looked at the impact conversations had on team performance. They measured impact by looking at profit and loss, customer satisfaction, and 360° reviews. They listened in on team conversations and calculated the ratio of positive to negative interactions, inquiry versus advocacy statements, and a focus on self versus others. The results were profound (see Table 6.1). A 6:1 ratio for high performance teams is a prescription for effective group dynamics. It is also not surprising, given the scientific research on neurophysiology and performance.

Table 6.1 Results of Losada and Heaphy's Research

Type of Talk	High-Performance Teams	Low-Performance Teams
Positive to Negative	6 to 1	1 to 20
Inquiry vs. Advocacy	1 to 1	1 to 3
Self vs. Other	1 to 1	30 to 1

This link between our interactions and the outcomes is true not only at work. John Gottman's research on what makes a marriage succeed suggests that there is a *magic ratio* of 5 to 1, positive to negative interactions. He found that marriages are significantly more likely to succeed when the couple's interactions are near that 5:1 ratio of positive to negative. When the ratio approaches 1:1, marriages move rapidly toward divorce.[19]

Gottman tested his *magic ratio* by predicting a couple's future, based on their interactions. In 1992, he videotaped a fifteen-minute conversation between each member of 700 couples, counting the number of positive and negative interactions. He followed up with each couple ten years later. He had predicted divorce with 94 percent accuracy![20] If we were to overhear fifteen minutes of conversation among *your* team members or family, what might we predict?

In addition to strengthening relationships and giving us greater access to our broader capacity, Appreciative Inquiry–based conversations invite meaningful engagement and often lead to action that gives us a sense of accomplishment. Martin Seligman, who is frequently credited with initiating this domain of psychology,[21] sees the topic of positive psychology as "well-being, that the gold standard for well-being is flourishing, and the goal of positive psychology is to increase flourishing."[22] Seligman suggests that the pathway to flourishing is to increase positive emotion, engagement, meaning, positive relationships, and achievement (PERMA).[23] These are metrics associated with conversations worth having. If you aspire to helping your organization flourish, one pathway is to ensure that the nature of the workplace conversations you have are predominantly appreciative and inquiry-based.

If you want strong relationships, high-performance teams, and a successful organization, then simply use the two basic AI practices. The research underscores the importance of having worthwhile or affirming conversations *most of the time*. It does not mean all the time. There are going to be negative interactions and situations that result in negative emotions. That's okay. Fredrickson's research suggests that a 3:1 positive to negative ratio is sufficient to maintain positivity. Losada and Heaphy's research showed that a 6:1 ratio is needed for high-performance teams. And Gottman says it is 5:1 for successful relationships. The point in understanding these various results is that we should maintain a healthy imbalance between positive and negative interactions. Remember Elizabeth and Ram's first reaction to Kamal when he told them there was a problem? They felt embarrassed for not being "good enough." What enabled them to rise to the occasion rather than collapsing in despair was the resilience they had built from many positive interactions, plus Kamal's Appreciative Inquiry–based approach to jointly creating a solution. We recommend aiming for a 4:1 ratio. This is a ratio with which we are all familiar: the 80/20 rule.[24]

Whether you are inspired by the compelling stories in this book or convinced by scientific evidence, or both, it is clear that if you want to inspire the best in human nature, it makes sense for you to practice positive framing and generative questioning. The bottom line is that conversations worth having are within your reach. You can intentionally expand your capacity to thrive, even in an uncertain world. In our last chapter, you'll see how it's possible to do precisely that, any time, any place, and in any situation.

7

Any Time, Any Place, Any Situation

Your conversations help create your world. Speak of delight, not dissatisfaction. Speak of hope, not despair. Let your words bind up wounds, not cause them.
— *Tao Te Ching*

Appreciative Inquiry is a strengths-based approach used to discover the best in people, organizations, and the communities around them. AI research has shown that systems (of self, teams, organizations, and communities) move in the direction of the questions people ask. AI initiates positive emotions and opens the doorway to unimagined possibilities for those who experience this way of being in and making sense of the world. This way of being is perhaps best described by Jane Magruder Watkins, a senior AI practitioner, OD consultant, and author, who says AI is "a habit of mind, heart, and imagination that searches for the success, the life-giving force rather than disaster and despair."[1] Starting appreciative and inquiry-based conversations is basically a matter of learning two simple practices: applying positive framing and using generative questions. When following the AI principles becomes second nature, you yourself will naturally initiate productive and meaningful interactions most of the time.

Getting Started with the Basic Practices

One place to begin is to observe conversations at home and at work. Try this exercise for a day before you start intentionally practicing positive framing and generative questions (though it might be hard to stop yourself if you've read this far!):

1. Get an index card and label one side "positive" and the reverse side "negative." After each conversation you observe or have (regardless of how long or short, and whether you are observing others or having a conversation with yourself or someone else), put a tick mark on the side representing whether it was an appreciative (positive) or a depreciative (negative) conversation. If it was a conversation you participated in, jot down a couple of words to remind yourself of how you felt during and after the interaction and whether it was worthwhile overall. If it was a conversation you observed, write down a few notes about where you were and what the tone and the direction of the interaction were. Note your observation of people's body language.
2. At the end of the day, reflect on your conversations and also those you observed. You might also reflect on how you feel about the day and what you've accomplished.
3. You can calculate your positivity ratio by adding up the total positive vs. negative conversations you had. If your ratio is less than 3:1, it's time to change your conversations. Fortunately, there's a simple way to do that!

If you're an effective problem-solver, you've probably been rewarded for that quality throughout your life. We are not suggesting that you give up this very effective skill. Rather, we ask you to be aware of when an appreciative approach might be more effective. We invite you to experience the difference between finding a solution using a more traditional problem-solving approach and using an appreciative approach. To confirm the power of this comparison, try the following exercise several times today or tomorrow:

1. When you are with people, consciously identify problems. Come up with solutions or ask problem-solving questions. Observe others' reactions and responses. Problem-solving questions typically entail asking about what's wrong, what's not working, and why. Notice the dynamics of these conversations. Observe subtle body language, as well as the tone and direction of the conversation. Along these same lines, if someone presents you with a problem, begin brainstorming solutions and notice how the conversation flows.

2. Then, consciously change to positive framing and ask generative questions. Positive framing flips the problem to a desired outcome. Generative questions seek to uncover what's working, what's going well, what's of value in a situation, what might be of value, what's possible, and what's desired. If someone else suggests the problem, ask them a generative question to flip the focus—for example, "This project is never going to work with the way it's designed." A generative question might instead be "What changes could we make so it *would* work?" Again, notice what happens to the dynamics of the conversation. Pay attention to changes in body language, the energy level, and the

tone and direction of the conversation. This can be especially powerful when someone presents you with a problem they are trying to solve. It might be helpful to first find out what they really want.

3. What emotions and feelings do these different ways of engaging in conversations generate—for you and for others? If you're a great problem-solver, such conversations might be energizing for you. What about others in the conversation? Which of these approaches builds stronger relationships among everyone? Makes room for everyone? Inspires the most innovative solutions?

The following are examples of ways people engage in conversation both before and after they learn about the two practices. Which ones are conversations worth having?

With Yourself

Before: Why didn't I get more accomplished today? How will I ever get this done if I don't take it home? I am exhausted but need to bring the report home with me. I am so tired of working at home every night. It's got to get done, and there's no one else to help me and no way I'll be ready for the meeting at 10 a.m.

After: I need to get this report finished by tomorrow, and today is gone! How can I be the most effective and efficient in knocking this thing out by 10 a.m. tomorrow? What will it take to finish it? I can just get here early tomorrow morning; that will do it!

With Your Partner/Spouse

Before: I'm not happy. You're always exhausted, and I'm tired of just watching TV. Why don't we ever do anything?

After: You know, we used to do more things together, and I really loved those times. I miss them. Remember when we…. What would it take to start doing some of those things again?

With Your Children

Before: Why aren't you home on time? You've got to stop getting in so late at night after curfew. Perhaps grounding you for a week is what you need!

After: I really need you to be in by curfew. We have good reasons for wanting you home by that time. Not to mention that I worry when you don't make it in. Sometimes you *do* manage to get here on time. What is it about those occasions that enables you to get home on time? How can we make sure that happens more often? I want to know you are safe. What can we both do to make sure I don't worry if you're running late?

With Colleagues

Before: These missed deadlines are a real problem for the department. Why are you late? If you can't do the work, we can give it to someone who can.

After: Do you agree that when we get our projects accomplished efficiently and on time we're in a better position to achieve our goals? What do you need to help you make sure your work on the project is completed on time?

With Government

Before: Why is there so much divisiveness between our citizens?

After: Which organizations are working to bridge the divide in this country? How can we bring that activity to our own community?

Simply altering the way in which you frame a situation and the questions you ask will change any interaction *and* the outcome. To generate big change and worthwhile outcomes, positive framing and generative questions have proven themselves, even in the most difficult of situations. At the time of our writing this book, many seeds of division and negativity are being sown into our national and global conversations. It is our hope that you might become a sower of conversations worth having in your communities and workplaces, especially across the polar divides that have emerged. This is where practicing positive framing and asking generative questions can actually begin to mend and even strengthen the fabric of our communities and nations, within and across our borders.

This may mean looking for the opportunity or the means to bring out the best even in a bad situation. It may also mean asking, "What is of value in this terrible thing that happened?" It may require first that you reflect on your own beliefs and ways of understanding, and then that you open the door for something new and meaningful to emerge. The AI principles will guide you here.

Playing by the Rules

Principles are "fundamental rules or truths that have application across the wide field of human interaction and engagement."[2] The principles introduced in chapter 4 are true, whether we are aware of them or not. They are true, regardless of our actions. They can be predictive of the outcomes of our actions. Their predictive nature is what makes them valuable. When we become aware of the principles, we can use them to enhance our ability to foster meaningful engagement.

You are likely to first bump up against the principles as you start to practice positive framing and generative questions. If you recall, Ravi at the tech company in India had a positive frame and asked generative questions, yet he ended up in a depreciative conversation. He bumped up against the principles—the rules. Successful application of the practices means following these principles to help you align your thoughts and feelings with your framing, language, and desired outcomes. Remember the following about the AI principles:

Constructionist Principle: Understanding, interpersonal dynamics, and ultimately reality are created through language and conversation. Playing by this rule means:

- Reflecting on the meaning you are bringing to an interaction
- Choosing to hold your viewpoint lightly and staying open
- Choosing words that allow for the creation of new meaning and understanding with others

Simultaneity Principle: Change happens the moment a question is asked or a statement is made. Playing by this rule means:

- Being mindful of your words, and choosing language that aligns with your intentions

- Paying attention to how your words are affecting yourself and others
- Asking generative questions to clarify other people's intention behind their words, instead of simply reacting to them

Poetic Principle: Every person, organization, or situation can be seen and understood from many perspectives. Playing by this rule means:

- Staying open and avoiding judgment
- Recognizing that what you are focused on is only part of the picture
- Attending to possibilities (instead of delving deeply into "fixing" things), moments of joy (instead of ruminating on fear or worry), and sources of energy and momentum (instead of inertia)
- Recognizing that you have a choice in how you interpret what happens in your life

Anticipatory Principle: The images and thoughts we hold influence our conversation and affect the future. Playing by this rule means:

- Expecting positive outcomes
- Anticipating what you want, instead of fearing what you *don't* want
- Looking for the opportunity, the good, the true, and the beautiful

Positive Principle: The more positive and generative the questions, the more positive and long-lasting the outcomes will be. Playing by this rule means:

- Asking bold, generative questions that elicit strong, affirmative images of possibility

These principles reinforce the idea that everything we think, say, and do moves us and those around us in one way or another. These principles underscore and drive our conversations, whether we realize it or not. Aligning our thoughts and feelings with a positive frame enables generative questions to flow naturally.

In any situation, you have many possible options to use positive framing and pose generative questions. You can ask questions that generate ideas or best practices, seek clarity and understanding, solicit personal strengths, or search for times when something is working well or someone seems at their best.

From everyday personal life challenges to even complex challenges at work and in communities, practicing positive framing and generative questions, informed by the AI principles, is an excellent way to sustain conversations worth having and to fuel productive and meaningful engagement.

The Next Conversation

This book has been about increasing opportunities as well as our sense of aliveness, creativity, meaning, and joy by intentionally engaging in conversations worth having. We can do this by using two simple practices and playing by the AI rules. As David Cooperrider remarks, "It is in the depth of our connections and conversations with others that we change ourselves and our relationships, one conversation at a time."[3] In this final chapter, we emphasize the key learnings that come alive in the stories we have shared:

- Ideas, words, and actions have impact. Be mindful how you use them in your conversations so that they have the impact you want.
- Conversations create images, which in turn create the blueprint for our future. Create the most positive images by asking the most generative questions. They are compelling.
- You always have many options for a conversation (critical, destructive, affirmative, and great). Make choices that generate conversations worth having.
- Nothing is static. Everything is dynamic and fluid. It's not about you. And it's not about the other. Rather, it's about the intersection of the two—*the conversation*—that can change in a heartbeat.

At times, we—the authors—still find ourselves caught up in *"ain't it awful?"* conversations. We still point out what's wrong with things. When we become more aware, we shake our heads and remember that we are still learning new habits to induce productive and meaningful engagement. Only then can we release the self-criticism that holds us back. We encourage you to have this compassion for yourself—as well as for others who join you in this adventure.

If you made it this far in the book, you know what it takes to engage in conversations worth having. Changing how you frame situations or ask questions will, of course, not happen overnight. However, with commitment and daily practice, you will experience the positive impact, and ultimately this way of being will actually *become* you. Committing yourself to conversations worth having will change your life, your work, and your world. These kinds of conversations have the potential to create big change. This change will influence your life *and* the world for the better.

Our final story tells how AI can turn even the most difficult conversation into one that is worthwhile. This story was written by Jackie's daughter, Ally, and describes her experience, at the age of thirteen, shortly after the family's three-week hiking vacation was unexpectedly canceled.[4] Ally's story shows us that we can ask life-giving questions even in not-so-life-giving moments. She began:

> *Every conversation is a series of defining moments that shape and change us.*

Things started off perfectly the day before we left, except that my dad had been complaining about stomach pain. I selfishly hoped this would not affect our vacation. The afternoon before our trip, I learned how drastically wrong I was. The trip was immediately canceled.

My dad was diagnosed with stage four lymphoma. He had a 50 percent chance of surviving. He was in the hospital for most of the summer. My mom stayed with him the entire time. This was the first time without our parents. My younger brother, Adam, and I were shuffled from relative to relative and could only visit my dad once a week for a short amount of time.

I was terrified of what might happen. I had no idea what I was going to do if he was suddenly ripped away. I tried to have a brave face, but I was scared. I thought, "What if the chemotherapy won't work, and what if he might die?" I tried to push these thoughts in my mind away, but these thoughts were there all the time. During the day, I went through the motions—I smiled when people talked to me and nodded like I was listening, but I really was not there. I never heard what people said to me. I walked around appearing normal on the outside but scared and confused on the inside.

I remember asking my mom, "Is Dad going to die?" I wanted her to say, "No, Ally, everything will be fine." She did not; she said, "Ally, we are all going to die someday, but for now we just have to stay positive and appreciate what is." But that was it—no assurance my dad would be fine. At the time, this was hard to swallow, because all I wanted her to say was that my dad was going to be just fine. That wasn't the answer I was looking for, but, strangely, it gave me some comfort. My mom trusted me enough to tell me the truth.

I remember the conversation with my mom. "How can I appreciate what is? This whole situation stinks," I blurted out. "Yes, it does, honey," she responded, acknowledging my feelings. Then, my mom did what she always does when I am sad or frustrated: She changed the conversation. "Tell me about your favorite moment with your dad," she asked, as if it were the most natural question in the world. Caught off guard again for a minute, I had to stop and think. I said, "I like when Dad and I are in the kitchen baking and playing our favorite music."

"Ally, what else do you like most about your dad?" she asked with a heart-filled smile. That was easy. I said, "I like how he sits on the front porch with me and we watch the sun go down."

"Yes, I like that too," she mused. "What do you think your dad likes most about you?"

"I think he likes how I make him laugh," I said, smiling inwardly as I suddenly had a mental image of my dad spitting milk out of his mouth after I made him laugh.

"Oh, yes, he definitely likes the way you make him laugh," my mother assured. "I'll tell you what, Ally: Tonight I want you to sit on the porch and watch the sun go down. While you are doing that, I will push your dad up to the hospital window, and we will watch it too. This is perfect; our front porch faces east to the hospital and your dad's hospital window faces west to our house. That way you

can both be watching the sun set, just from different places. How does that sound?" she asked.

"Yes, Mom, I think I would like that," I answered, feeling strange that suddenly I was looking forward to the coming evening. She gave me a hug, and I watched her drive away again back to the hospital. As she drove away, I found myself smiling again, thinking about what a great conversation we had in such a bad time.

Now, as I look back on the talks we had, I realized my mom's secret formula was that she was always honest with me. She never told me "Things are going to be fine" or "It will all be back to normal soon." I knew that if my mom said it, then it was the truth and not just something to make me feel better. At first, it felt a little like this was just being positive, but then I realized these conversations were about what is, what could be, and what might be. I truly learned to focus on the things about my dad that could help him get through his treatments and regain his desire for living. Now, three years later, my dad is back at work, and we are watching the sunset from our porch again. AI helped us get through the dark moments, helping us draw on our strengths and restoring our faith. It was a lesson that was hard to grasp as a thirteen-year-old, but I was fortunate—I grew up in a household that embraced the ideals of Appreciative Inquiry for my entire life.

This experience really changed me, because I learned to live with an appreciative mindset. Drawing on AI in desperate times at first did not make sense to me. I cannot tell you that I am a better person because of it, but I can tell you that I am a different person. It was a turning point for me—a time when my thinking shifted from "what about me?" to "what can I do to help my parents and others?" I learned to accept responsibility and to cope with the idea of potentially losing someone I will love forever. I hope that I never have to go through this again, but if I do I know where and how to start the conversation.

This story has a positive ending. Paul, her father, is doing great. He is in remission, and the life of everyone in her family has returned to a "new normal." Ally gets to be a teenager again, but now she's an appreciative one. She learned how to handle a tough situation through the power of inquiry from an Appreciative Inquiry perspective. She shared: *"I learned to be appreciative, have faith, and not lose hope. Today, I look at situations with an appreciative lens, which is easy to do when things are going well but quite the challenge when things are not. I try to see what is good and what can be in just about any situation, and most of all appreciate what I have."*

Ally's story illustrates how all of us can have a sense of well-being and joy at difficult times. Using both appreciation and inquiry are the most essential concepts in creating powerfully positive conversations worth having. Recall the stories we have shared with you and how each person in them learned to create a positive shift. They simply practiced positive framing and asked generative questions. The resulting conversations invited engagement and produced positive outcomes. They created environments in which people could show up as their best selves. Human systems are either degenerating or growing and evolving toward the future. Why not make it a future that has the potential to work for everyone? We are offering a simple way to do precisely that.

Writing this book has been a humbling and collaborative learning process. Most of the time, we engaged in productive and meaningful conversations about our work. There were, of course, moments when we disagreed or diverged on an idea. Coming back to practice what we were writing about at these challenging moments proved to be an amazing experience. We discovered that it is truly delightful when something simple works so well. Plus, we have been helped immensely along our journey by engaging those in our communities: family members; Berrett-Koehler (our publisher); colleagues; and friends.

As we mentioned at the outset, we consider ourselves continuous learners in this adventure called life. We want to hear your questions, comments, thoughts, suggestions, and ideas for starting and sustaining conversations worth having in your life. Please visit our website,

www.conversationsworthhaving.today

to share your own stories about how you are generating positive change.

There are many possible worlds out there. The probability that any one of them comes into being depends on our conversations. What kind of conversations will *you* have next?

Notes

Introduction

1. See Dee Hock, *One from Many: Visa and the Rise of the Chaordic Organization* (San Francisco: Berrett-Koehler, 2005). Also see Fast Company's *The Trillion-Dollar Vision of Dee Hock: The Corporate Radical Who Organized Visa Wants to Dis-organize Your Company*, 1996. The opening quotes come from personal conversation.
2. Peter Senge, Foreword, in Hock, *One from Many*.
3. David Cooperrider, "The Gift of New Eyes: Personal Reflections on Appreciative Inquiry into Organizational Life," in A. Shani et al., eds., *Research in Organizational Change and Development*, vol. 25 (Bingley, UK: Emerald, 2017).
4. In the world of Appreciative Inquiry (AI), the term "positive" means not an answer but rather a question. It invites an appreciative *search* for the true, the good, the better, and the possible—literally, everything that "gives life" and those things of value worth valuing. AI is about the search for "what gives life" to living-systems organizations, communities, industries, countries, families, networks, societies, relationships, and our global living systems when they are most alive and jointly flourishing in their inseparable and intimate inter-relations. AI's generativity lies precisely in its "inquiry inspired by life" North Star and in its starting the search not in current ideals (certainties) but in the lure of unexplored possibilities (those intimations of something more) where possibility and positive potential can be sensed in the texture of the actual—searching for our world's life-giving best, in moments that are *extraordinary* (positive deviations) in moments that are *ordinary* (like a Van Gogh seeing the essence in a teapot or other "ordinary" things), and even in high meaning-making moments often involving *tragedy* (see Victor Frankl's *Man's Search for Meaning*). So, when you see the word "positive," think not of answers but of the depth search for what gives life, in this setting and context, something beyond our current knowledge where "inquiry is the experience of mystery, that changes our lives." Taken together, where appreciation and inquiry are wonderfully entangled, we experience knowledge that's not inert but alive, as well

as an ever-expansive inauguration of our world to new possibilities. In many ways, I've begun to question today whether there can even *be* inquiry where there is no appreciation, valuing, or amazement, or what the Greeks called *thaumazein*—the borderline between wonderment and admiration. This volume does a wonderful job of making the principles and practices of AI come alive, in easily applicable ways, thus empowering everyday vital conversation.

Chapter 1 Shifting Conversations

1. Ironically, the first AI application was the Cleveland Clinic Story, by David Cooperrider and Suresh Srivastva, "Appreciative Inquiry in Organizational Life," in W. A. Pasmore and R. Woodman, *Research in Organization Change and Development* (Greenwich, CT: JAI Press, 1987), 129–69.
2. To learn more about Appreciative Inquiry, visit the AI Commons, https://appreciativeinquiry.champlain.edu, a worldwide portal devoted to the fullest sharing of academic resources and practical tools about Appreciative Inquiry and the rapidly growing discipline of positive change.

Chapter 2 What Kind of Conversations Are You Having?

1. Jeffrey Ford and Laurie Ford, *The Four Conversations: Daily Conversations that Get Results* (San Francisco: Berrett-Koehler, 2009), 201. Their work focuses on four types of conversations in the workplace: initiative, understanding, performance, and closure.
2. Barbara Fredrickson, "The Role of Positive Emotions in Positive Psychology: The Broaden-and-Build Theory of Positive Emotions," *American Psychologist* 56, no. 3 (2001): 218–26.
3. Barbara Fredrickson, *Positivity* (New York: JMF Books, 2009).
4. Martin Seligman is a pioneer in the positive psychology field, which focuses on well-being and human flourishing. To learn more about how this field developed, visit www.pursuit-of-happiness.org/history-of-happiness/martin-seligman-psychology/.
5. Barbara Fredrickson, "What Good Are Positive Emotions?" *Rev. General Psychology* 2, no. 30 (September 1998): 300–319.
6. A futures institute is typically a nonprofit research organization dedicated to developing practical tools, research, and programs that help people make the future—today. These institutes track signals, create maps and artifacts, and bring people together to think critically about responding in a world of continuous and rapid change. These institutes collaborate with one another, working to provide foresight for our future.
7. Gervase Bushe, "Generative Process, Generative Outcomes: The Transformational Potential of Appreciative Inquiry," in D. L. Cooperrider et al., eds., *Organizational Generativity: The Appreciative Inquiry Summit and a Scholarship of Transformation*, vol. 4, *Advances in Appreciative Inquiry* (Bingley, UK: Emerald, 2013), 89–113.
8. Empirical studies confirm that this produces a positive climate and significantly higher performance. Kim Cameron, *Positive Leadership* (San Francisco: Berrett-Koehler, 2012), and the Center for Positive Organizations; see http://positiveorgs.bus.umich.edu.

9. Examples of this are presented by Harlene Anderson, *Conversation, Language, and Possibilities: A Postmodern Approach to Therapy* (New York: Basic Books, 1997). Anderson explores the question of how therapists and clients can create relationships and conversations that allow both parties to access possibilities where none seemed to exist before. She emphasizes the importance of "therapist and client engaging in *collaborative relationships* and *generative conversations* to form *conversational partnerships* toward powerful transformations in people's lives and toward successful futures."

10. Marilee Adams has written two books on question thinking. She proposes two paradigms of questioning—the judger and the learner—and details how best to shift from the judger paradigm to the learner paradigm. For further reading: Marilee Adams, *Change Your Questions, Change Your Life* (San Francisco: Berrett-Koehler, 2004), and also her first book, *The Art of the Question: A Guide to Short-Term Question-Centered Therapy* (New York: Wiley, 1998).

11. Barbara Fredrickson's research indicates that we need a minimum of a 3:1 ratio of positive emotions to negative emotions in order to stay healthy and vital. Fredrickson, *Positivity*. Marcial Losada and Emily Heaphy's research shows that high-performing teams actually have a 6:1 ratio: "The Role of Positivity and Connectivity in the Performance of Business Teams: A Nonlinear Dynamics Model," *American Behavioral Scientist* 47, no. 6 (February 2004): 740–65.

12. Barbara Fredrickson, "The Value of Positive Emotions," *American Scientist* 91, no. 4 (2003): 330–34.

13. Losada and Heaphy, "The Role of Positivity and Connectivity in the Performance of Business Teams." John Gottman, *What Makes Marriages Succeed or Fail* (New York: Simon & Schuster, 1994).

14. Feedforward is the practice of giving appreciative feedback by answering two questions: (1) What do you like about the idea, project, proposal, or plan?; and (2) What suggestions do you have for making it even better?

Chapter 3 Two Simple Appreciative Practices

1. Gervase Bushe, "Appreciative Inquiry Is Not (Just) About the Positive," *OD Practitioner* 39, no. 4 (2007): 30–35.

2. The term "flip" has been used by many to describe how to shift from negative to positive. Thomas H. White, former president of GTE Telephone Operations, referenced the "flip-side of the coin" when describing using AI in his organization in David L. Cooperrider, Diana Whitney, Jacqueline M. Stavros, *Appreciative Inquiry Handbook*, p. xx (Bedford Heights, OH: Lakeshore, 2003). Diana Whitney, Amanda Trosten-Bloom, and Kae Rader describe "the flip" in *Appreciative Leadership* (San Francisco: McGraw-Hill, 2010), 35–41, and Jeremy McCarthy refers to "the positive flip" in http://psychologyofwellbeing.com. Over the years, this shift has been referred to as "the flip" in the AI community or "the positive flip" in the positive psychology community.

3. Bushe, "Generative Process, Generative Outcomes."

4. Chip Heath and Dan Heath, *Switch* (New York: Broadway Books, 2010).

5. Gretchen Spreitzer and Scott Sonenshein define a positive deviance as something that represents "intentional behaviors that depart from the norm of a reference group in honorable ways." Thus, it reaches a "level of positive deviance that extends beyond achieving effectiveness or ordinary success (p. 209); see

"Positive Deviance and Extraordinary Performance," in K. S. Cameron, J. E. Dutton, and R. E. Quinn, eds., *Positive Organizational Scholarship: Foundations of a New Discipline* (San Francisco: Berrett-Koehler, 2003), 207–24.

6. For more information on transformative talk about how to reflect and reframe with positive intent, see Robert J. Marshak, "Generative Conversations: How to Use Deep Listening and Transforming Talk in Coaching and Consulting," *Organization Development Practitioner 56*, no. 3 (2004): 25–29.

7. Fredrickson, "The Value of Positive Emotions," 330–34.

Chapter 4 What's Driving Your Conversations?

1. Under the guidance of Suresh Srivastva, David Cooperrider created the original AI principles. These principles were first published by Cooperrider and Srivastva in "Appreciative Inquiry in Organizational Life," W. A. Pasmore and R. Woodman, eds., *Research in Organization Change and Development* (Greenwich, CT: JAI Press, 1987), 129–69.

2. For a deeper dive into the AI principles and how they govern and affect our action and relationships, see Jacqueline M. Stavros and Cheri Torres, *Dynamic Relationships: Unleashing the Power of Appreciative Inquiry in Daily Living* (Chagrin Falls, OH: Taos Institute Publishing, 2005).

3. For more detailed information on AI systematic discovery of what gives life to a system, see David Cooperrider, Diana Whitney, and Jacqueline M. Stavros, *The Appreciative Inquiry Handbook*, 2nd ed. (San Francisco: Berrett-Koehler, 2008).

4. By "constructionist" we are referring to social constructionism, which is a theory of knowledge grounded in the idea that we jointly (that is, socially) construct meaning and understanding about the world based on our experience and shared assumptions. We create models of the social world, then we share and reify those models through language. The foremost leaders in social constructionist theory and practice are members of the Taos Institute. You will find further information and resources at www.taosinstitute.net.

5. Ropes courses, also called challenge courses, comprise a set of activities that require significant teamwork and shared leadership for success. Typically, these courses are built in the woods. Outward Bound popularized such courses.

6. Cheri Torres, *The Appreciative Facilitator: A Handbook for Teachers and Facilitators* (Asheville, NC: Collaborative by Design, 2001).

7. The Poetic Principle says, "Our lives are like an open book or a poem that is constantly being written, and rewritten, read and reinterpreted. We can find new meaning in old story lines when we ask different questions." In Stavros and Torres, *Dynamic Relationships*, 66.

8. David L. Cooperrider, "Positive Image,Positive Action: The Affirmative Basis of Organizing," in Suresh Srivastva and David L. Cooperrider, *Appreciative Management and Leadership*, rev. ed. (Euclid, OH: Lakeshore Communications, 1999), 91–125.

Chapter 5 Scaling Up Great Conversations

1. Visit the AI Commons to see illustrations of cities, countries, organizations, and global initiatives around the world that use the AI 5-D Cycle, available at https://appreciativeinquiry.champlain.edu/.

2. To read the Fairmount Santrol story, visit www.youtube.com/watch?v= eGOvgFoDZaY.

3. Jenniffer Deckard, keynote speaker, "How Appreciative Inquiry Contributes to a Culture of Do Good, Do Well," Flourishing Conference, June 16, 2017, Cleveland, OH.

4. For more in-depth information about the AI 5-D Cycle in organizations, see Diana Whitney and Amanda Trosten-Bloom, *The Power of Appreciative Inquiry*, and David L. Cooperrider, Diana Whitney, and Jacqueline M. Stavros, *The Appreciative Inquiry Handbook* (Euclid, OH: Lakeshore Publishers, 2005).

5. For more information on using AI to create strategy and strategic plans, see Jacqueline M. Stavros and Gina Hinrichs, *The Thin Book of SOAR: Building Strengths-Based Strategy* (Bend, OR: Thin Book, 2009), or visit www. soar-strategy.com.

Chapter 6 It's Not Magic, It's Science!

1. Margaret Wheatley, *Leadership and the New Science: Discovering Order in a Chaotic World* (San Francisco: Berrett-Koehler, 2006).

2. Positive psychology is defined as "the scientific study of what makes life worth living." Christopher Peterson, "What Is Positive Psychology and What Is It Not?" *Psychology Today* (May 16, 2008), www.psychologytoday.com/ blog/the-good-life/200805/what-is-positive-psychology-and-what-is-it-not (accessed August 7, 2017). It is further defined as "the scientific study of positive human functioning and flourishing on multiple levels that include the biological, personal, relational, institutional, cultural, and global dimensions of life." Martin Seligman and Mihaly Csikszentmihalyi, "Positive Psychology: An Introduction," *American Psychologist* 55, no. 1 (2000): 5–14.

3. David Cooperrider, "The Concentration Effect of Strengths: How the Whole System AI Summits Bring Out the Best in Human Enterprise," *Organizational Dynamics* 41 (2012): 106–17.

4. University of California, Los Angeles, "New UCLA Imaging Study First to Show Placebo Alters Brain Function in Individuals with Major Depression," *Science Daily*, www.sciencedaily.com/releases/2002/01/020102074543.htm (accessed June 19, 2016).

5. Doc Childre and Howard Martin, *The HeartMath Solution* (New York: HarperCollins, 1999).

6. Ibid.

7. Cooperrider, "Positive Image, Positive Action," 93–95, 106.

8. Tania Lombrozo, "The Truth about the Right Brain/Left Brain Relationship," www.npr.org/sections/13.7/2013/12/02/248089436/the-truth-about-the-left-brain-right-brain-relationship (accessed June 19, 2016), and Evelyn Virschup and Bernard Virschup, *Visual Imagery: The Language of the Right Brain* (Los Angeles: University of Southern California School of Medicine, 1980).

9. Daniel S. Kirschenbaum, Arnold M. Tomarken, and Robert Holtzbauer, "Effects of Differential Self-Monitoring and Level of Mastery on Sports Performance: Brain Power Bowling," *Cognitive Therapy and Research* 6, no, 3 (1982): 335–42.

10. Cooperrider, "Positive Image, Positive Action," 109.

11. Cooperrider, "Positive Image, Positive Action," 95–96, and "The Power of the Placebo Effect," *Harvard Health Publications,* at www.health.harvard.edu/mental-health/the-power-of-the-placebo-effect (accessed August 6, 2017).
12. Robert Rosenthal, "Interpersonal Expectancy Effects: A 30-Year Perspective," *Current Directions in Psychological Sciences* 3, no. 6 (December 1994): 176–79, and Jane Elliott, "A Class Divided," *PBS Frontline,* www.pbs.org/wgbh/pages/frontline/shows/divided_(accessed August 6, 2017).
13. Cooperrider, "Positive Image, Positive Action," 92–102.
14. Peale was a hugely influential popularizer of the power of positive thinking in the U.S. Zigler was a highly successful salesperson, motivational speaker, and trainer; he wrote more than twelve books and influenced the lives of millions of people with his positive messages and encouraging words.
15. Fredrickson, "The Broaden-and-Build Theory of Positive Emotions."
16. Ibid., 218–26.
17. Fredrickson, *Positivity.*
18. Losada and Heaphy, "The Role of Positivity and Connectivity in the Performance of Business Teams."
19. Gottman, *What Makes Marriages Succeed or Fail.*
20. Ibid.
21. For a brief but complete overview of the history of positive psychology, see T. S. Srinivasan, "The Five Founding Fathers and a History of Positive Psychology," *Positive Psychology Program* (February 12, 2015), available at https://positivepsychologyprogram.com/founding-fathers/ (accessed August 7, 2017).
22. Martin Seligman, *Flourish: A Visionary New Understanding of Happiness and Well-being* (New York: Free Press, 2011), 13.
23. Ibid., 16–18.
24. Cooperrider, "The Concentration Effect of Strengths."

Chapter 7 Any Time, Any Place, Any Situation

1. Jane Watkins was instrumental in bringing AI into organization-life in hundreds of organizations in more than fifty countries. Jane Magruder Watkins, Bernard Mohr, and Ralph Kelly, *Appreciative Inquiry: Change at the Speed of Imagination,* 2nd ed. (San Francisco: Pfeiffer, 2011).
2. Neil Samuels and Cheri Torres, in collaboration with the Appreciative Governance Team, "Organizational Design Principles for Appreciative Governance," *The AI Practitioner* 13, no. 4 (November 2011): 24.
3. Stavros and Torres, *Dynamic Relationships,* 15.
4. This original, full story by Ally is in the issue Young Practitioners, Co-Creating the Future of Appreciative Inquiry, "Learning to Leverage Appreciative Inquiry in a Not So Appreciative Moment," *The Appreciative Inquiry Practitioner* 19, no. 1 (February 2017). It has been abridged here and updated by Ally as she recalls the conversation she had using AI in a difficult situation.

Bibliography

Adams, Marilee. *Change Your Questions, Change Your Life.* San Francisco: Berrett-Koehler, 2009.

Barrett, Frank, and Ron Fry. *Appreciative Inquiry: A Positive Approach to Building Cooperative Capacity.* Chagrin Falls, OH: Taos Institute, 2005.

Cooperrider, David L., and Suresh Srivastva. *Appreciative Management and Leadership: The Power of Positive Thought and Action in Organizations.* Euclid, OH: Williams Custom Publishing, 1999.

Cooperrider, David L., and Diana Whitney. *Appreciative Inquiry: A Positive Revolution in Change.* San Francisco: Berrett-Koehler, 2005.

Cooperrider, David L., Diana Whitney, and Jacqueline M. Stavros. *The Appreciative Inquiry Handbook.* San Francisco: Berrett-Koehler, 2008.

Ford, Jeffrey, and Laurie Ford. *The Four Conversations: Daily Communication That Gets Results.* San Francisco: Berrett-Koehler, 2009.

Fredrickson, Barbara. *Positivity: Top-Notch Research Reveals the Upward Spiral That Will Change Your Life.* New York: Crown, 2009.

Hammond, Sue. *The Thin Book of Appreciative Inquiry.* Bend, OR: Thin Book Publishing, 2013.

Ludema, James D., Diana Whitney, Bernard J. Mohr, and Thomas J. Griffin. *The Appreciative Inquiry Summit: A Practitioner's Guide for Leading Large-Group Change.* San Francisco: Berrett-Koehler, 2003.

Schiller, Marjorie, Bea Mah Holland, and Deanna Riley, eds. *Appreciative Leaders: In the Eye of the Beholder.* Chagrin Falls, OH: Taos Institute, 2001.

Seligman, Martin. *Flourish: A Visionary New Understanding of Happiness and Well-being.* New York: Free Press, 2011.

Stavros, Jacqueline M., and Gina Hinrichs. *The Thin Book of SOAR: Building Strengths-Based Strategy.* Bend, OR: Thin Book Publishing, 2009.

Stavros, Jacqueline M., and Cheri Torres. *Dynamic Relationships: Unleashing the Power of Appreciative Inquiry in Daily Living.* Chagrin Falls, OH: Taos Institute, 2005.

Thatchenkery, Tojo, and Carol Metzker. *Appreciative Intelligence: Seeing the Mighty Oak in the Acorn.* San Francisco: Berrett-Koehler, 2006.

Torres, Cheri. *The Appreciative Facilitator: A Handbook for Teachers and Facilitators.* Asheville, NC: Collaborative by Design, 2001.

Watkins, Jane Magruder, Bernard Mohr, and Ralph Kelly. *Appreciative Inquiry: Change at the Speed of Imagination,* 2nd ed. San Francisco: Pfeiffer, 2011.

Whitney, Diana, and Amanda Trosten-Bloom. *The Power of Appreciative Inquiry: A Practical Guide to Positive Change.* San Francisco: Berrett-Koehler, 2003.

Acknowledgments

No book is the result of its authors alone, and ours is no different. Writing *Conversations Worth Having* emerged from conversation after conversation with one another and with our families, colleagues, friends, editor, and clients, many of whose stories we tell in these pages. We would be remiss if we did not acknowledge our fifteen years of friendship with each other and the complementary nature of our styles and temperaments, which brought balance and clarity to our collective writing. Our understanding of just how simple it is to engage in great conversations unveiled itself as we wrote. The foundation for our work, of course, is grounded in the brilliance and generosity of David Cooperrider and his colleagues at Case Western Reserve University. They have given a gift to the world that has blessed our lives and careers. A special thank-you to David for writing the Introduction—we are humbled by your words.

We also acknowledge, greatly appreciate, and thank other members of the AI community who helped to shape our understanding and practical application of Appreciative Inquiry: Frank Barrett, Gervase Bushe, Dawn Dole-Cooperrider, Ron Fry, Lindsey Godwin, Colette Herrick, Ralph Kelly, Sallie

Lee, Jane Magruder-Watkins, Mo McKenna, Bernard Mohr, Anne Radford, Dan Saint, Neil Samuels, Marge Schiller, David Shaked, Robyn Stratton-Berkessel, Amanda Trosten-Bloom, Diana Whitney, and Joep de Yong. As well, we thank Ken Gergen and the Taos Institute associates for their commitment to the field of social construction and their efforts to bring its application to the world. A special thanks to those we work with for all the many conversations worth having we've had over the years, which no doubt contributed to what appears in these pages: the appreciative trio at the Flourishing Leadership Institute (Jon Berghoff, Laura MacMinn, and Trent Schulz); members of Innovation Partners International (Mike Feinson, Lisa Hirsh, Bob Laliberte, Ada Jo Mann, Bernard Mohr, Christine Whitney Sanchez, and Bill Scott); Colette Herrick of Insight Shift; the leadership at the Center for Appreciative Inquiry/Company of Experts (Kathy Becker, Jim Pulliam, and Melissa Robiana); Tony and Jen Silbert of Spartina; and members of NextMove (Haiz Oppenheimer and Amelia Terrapin).

Along the way, we have had countless conversations about the book with others. They offered words of encouragement as well as valuable insights and feedback that helped shape our writing. These others include the Lawrence Technological University family of administration, staff, faculty, and students; the positive psychology and positivity community; the Center for Positive Organizations; Tammy Love and staff members at the Institute for Nuclear Power Operations; and the Reverend Sally Beth Shore and members of the Unitarian Universalist Church of Spartanburg, South Carolina.

We are also grateful to our clients, colleagues, friends, and family members for the stories that appear in the book. We have changed most of your names, but you no doubt recognized yourself in your story. Thank you for being an example and for sharing your story with us so that we can share it with others.

We would especially like to thank the members of our newest family—Berrett-Koehler Publishers. Named in the order in which we met them, we are deeply grateful to Jeevan Sivasubramaniam for his endless patience and for opening the door into BK. He waited many years until it was the right moment for our manuscript to come together. We love his thoughtful directness, sense of humor, and responsiveness.

We express gratitude also to Steve Piersanti, our editor, without whom this book would not be in your hands. His awareness of the power and impact that Appreciative Inquiry can have in the world made his work with us all the more potent. His knowledge and expertise, coupled with his thought-provoking questions, helped us simplify our message. We greatly appreciate his willingness to push back and then let us sit with ambiguity until we found our way to clarifying complex AI concepts.

We sincerely appreciate the time, care, and incredibly helpful recommendations given to us from our BK manuscript reviewers: Julie Clayton, Bette Krakau, Carol Metzker, and Chloe Park. Each of these insightful women made valuable contributions to the final manuscript. In addition, we are grateful for the time and editorial support given by Cecile Betit, Dan Casetta, and Ed Kimball. A special thank-you to Mark Levy for his inspiration, his writing tips, and the enthusiasm he continuously brought to our conversations.

We are grateful to the more than 500 people who gave us feedback on the book's title, making it very clear that *Conversations Worth Having* was a winner. Many thanks to Lasell Whipple and her production team; designing the cover was easy, thanks to Lasell and Adam Johnson, who translated our conversations about the cover into a vibrant, colorful design that everyone agreed on. Our gratitude to Steven Hiatt, our production editor and text designer, for his attention to detail and his aesthetic eye, and to our copyeditor, Mark Woodworth, and proofreader, Tom Hassett. And much appreciation for Courtney Schonfeld for making an audio version of our book available.

Our publishing family continued to grow as we met and collaborated with the remarkable and detail-focused marketing team. Much gratitude and appreciation for our team lead, Mike Crowley, as well as for María Jesús Aguiló, Shabnam Banerjee-McFarland, Leslie Crandell, Kristen Frantz, David Marshall, Liz McKellar, Katie Sheehan, Mayowa Tomori, and Johanna Vondeling. Thanks to them all for helping to bring the message in this book to the world. And a note of thanks to the BK Authors Group for providing workshops and retreats that enliven, uplift, and energize the BK author community. We are grateful to have the opportunity to connect with other authors and thankful for the support they are giving us. We are thrilled to be part of this community, and we commit to the same generosity we have been shown.

We are honored to be a part of the BK family, aligning our words and our work with their mission: *to create a world that works for all!* We are so grateful to be on this journey at this time in history with an organization as honorable as BK.

In closing, we express our gratitude for our families. Special thanks to our husbands, Paul Stavros and Michael Torres, who were loving, supportive, and encouraging even when writing took over our evenings and weekends. An extra note of gratitude to Paul for his enthusiasm and efforts to help us design cards and our website.

We are also deeply aware of how much our children have provided us opportunities to learn and to practice positive framing and generative questions, and to come up against the principles time and time again. They have kept us honest by asking generative questions when we were focused on what's wrong, reminding us to look for what is *right* with the world. Huge thank-yous to Ally, for her constant cheer and life-defining story in our final chapter, and to Adam, for his sense of humor and ability to take care of himself when writing consumed our time. Laura and Carmen, we are grateful for your encouragement, your joy in hearing about our work, and your reflection of all that is good, true, and beautiful in the world. To all of our children: We hope the conversations taking place in the world today begin to transform into conversations that generate a greener, more loving, inclusive, and human world that is safe and enlivening for you and *your* children . . . and your children's children for seven generations to come.

Index

About the David L. Cooperrider Center for Appreciative Inquiry

The David L. Cooperrider Center for Appreciative Inquiry is the global Center of Excellence for Appreciative Inquiry and strengths-based management practices. Based in the Robert P. Stiller School of Business at Champlain College in Burlington, Vermont, the Center is the first academic-based center focusing on advancing the theory and practice of Appreciative Inquiry (AI).

Its mission is to educate leaders to be the best *in* the world at seeing the best *for* the world, as well as to discover and design positive institutions, organizations, and communities that elevate, magnify, and bring our highest human strengths to the practice of positive organization development and change. To bring this mission to life, the Center provides education programs, applied practice, and global knowledge incubation. The Center's educational focus supports its overarching goal: to change the world, one appreciative leader at a time. Through its applied practice, the Center has created thriving partnerships with companies and organizations around the globe. It also partners with the International Positive Education Network

(IPEN) to convene the World Accelerator for Positive Education, aiming to advance positive education from early education on. Other key initiatives include:

- AI Certification program—champlain.edu/ai-home/appreciative-education
- AI Commons—https://appreciativeinquiry.champlain.edu
- Co-publication of the *AI Practitioner International Journal*—aipractitioner.com
- AI World Inquiry on AI impacts around the world—aiworldinquiry.com

The Center takes its name from Dr. David L. Cooperrider, the world-renowned thought leader on AI. The Center was made possible through a 2012 gift from Robert and Christine Stiller to Champlain College. To learn more, visit www.champlain.edu/appreciativeinquiry.

About the Authors

Jackie Stavros, DM. Jackie's passion is working with others to discover their strengths, identify opportunities, and create a plan with meaningful results for positive change. She is internationally recognized for her creation of SOAR, a positive approach to strategic thinking, plan-

ning, and leading that focuses on strengths, opportunities, and aspirations and that results in strategic conversations (www. soar-strategy.com). The heart of her work is using Appreciative Inquiry (AI), one of the most popular approaches to positive change—that is, bringing out the best in people, their organizations, and their communities to fuel *conversations worth having* that produce meaningful engagement and results.

Jackie has been integrating strengths-based, whole-system practices into her research, teaching, training, coaching, and consulting work to strengthen relationships, affect performance, and create positive change. She works with organizations in leadership development, team-building, and strategic planning. She helps them to identify and articulate their values, vision, mission, strategy, and strategic initiatives and then to build collaborative teams and communities for results-oriented action. She has worked across all sectors, including for-profit, nonprofit, government, and a wide spectrum of industries.

Jackie is a professor at Lawrence Technological University (LTU) College of Management, in Southfield, Michigan, and has been honored with the LTU Inaugural Presidential Research Award. She is Senior Appreciative Inquiry Strategist for Flourishing Leadership Institute and a member of the Appreciative Inquiry Council of Practitioners for the Cooperrider Center for Appreciative Inquiry and the Taos Institute. Before she joined LTU, her industry work included manufacturing, automotive, banking, technology, education, healthcare, government, and professional services. As a college student, her first professional position was as a sales rep for Cutco Cutlery, whose leaders planted in her a seed of positivity.

Jackie has coauthored many books, book chapters, and articles, including: *Appreciative Inquiry Handbook: For Leadership of Change; Dynamic Relationships: Unleashing the Power of Appreciative Inquiry in Daily Living;* and *Thin Book of SOAR: Building Strengths-Based Strategy.* She has presented her research and work in over 25 countries. She is a keynote speaker on AI, SOAR, and positive approaches to leadership development and change. Jackie earned her doctorate in management (DM) from Weatherhead School of Management at Case Western Reserve University. She earned an MBA at Michigan State University and a BA at Wayne State University. She lives in Brighton, Michigan, with her husband, Paul; their kids, Ally and Adam; and Rex, a lovable dog.

Cheri B. Torres, Ph.D.
Cheri's passion is helping people learn to transform their relationships, organizations, and communities by engaging in conversations worth having. She specializes in leadership and team development, emphasizing the art of productive and meaningful

engagement. Leaders working with her learn to create the kind of relational dynamics that ignite the full potential of their teams and organization, resulting in high performance, innovation, and goal achievement. She also partners with communities and organizations for whole-systems change and strategic planning, bringing all stakeholders together for planning, design, and collaborative action. She has worked across all sectors: corporate, government, education, and social profit/NGOs, supporting their capacity for learning and innovation, shared leadership, teamwork, and collective impact. She has trained thousands of trainers and teachers in the use and practice of Experiential Learning, Appreciative Inquiry, and other strengths-based processes. In addition to the United States, she has worked in Mexico, Canada, South America, Europe, and India.

In 2009, Cheri founded Collaborative by Design, reflecting her commitment to collaborate with clients and other consulting groups for positive change. She currently is a founding partner or an associate with a number of such groups, including Next-Move, Innovation Partners International, Insight Shift, the Taos Institute, the Center for Appreciative Inquiry, and UniteWNC.

Cheri holds a Ph.D. in educational psychology with a specialization in Collaborative Learning from the University of

Tennessee. She also holds an MBA, a Master's in Transpersonal Psychology, Level 2 certification in Cultural Transformation Tools/Barrett Values Centre, and Level II certification in Spiral Dynamics Integral. She has authored numerous books and articles, including *The Appreciative Facilitator: Accelerated Learning Practices* and *Dynamic Relationships: Unleashing the Power of Appreciative Inquiry in Daily Living.* She coauthored a chapter for the newest edition of *Advances in Appreciative Inquiry* and a chapter in *Appreciative Education.* She codesigned and patented Mobile Team Challenge, an award-winning, portable low-ropes course. She lives in Asheville, North Carolina, with her husband, Michael; their two dogs, Logan and Annabelle; and Ziggy and Lucy, their cats.

Berrett–Koehler
Publishers

Berrett-Koehler is an independent publisher dedicated to an ambitious mission: *Connecting people and ideas to create a world that works for all.*

We believe that the solutions to the world's problems will come from all of us, working at all levels: in our organizations, in our society, and in our own lives. Our BK Business books help people make their organizations more humane, democratic, diverse, and effective (we don't think there's any contradiction there). Our BK Currents books offer pathways to creating a more just, equitable, and sustainable society. Our BK Life books help people create positive change in their lives and align their personal practices with their aspirations for a better world.

All of our books are designed to bring people seeking positive change together around the ideas that empower them to see and shape the world in a new way.

And we strive to practice what we preach. At the core of our approach is Stewardship, a deep sense of responsibility to administer the company for the benefit of all of our stakeholder groups including authors, customers, employees, investors, service providers, and the communities and environment around us. Everything we do is built around this and our other key values of quality, partnership, inclusion, and sustainability.

This is why we are both a B-Corporation and a California Benefit Corporation—a certification and a for-profit legal status that require us to adhere to the highest standards for corporate, social, and environmental performance.

We are grateful to our readers, authors, and other friends of the company who consider themselves to be part of the BK Community. We hope that you, too, will join us in our mission.

A BK Life Book

BK Life books help people clarify and align their values, aspirations, and actions. Whether you want to manage your time more effectively or uncover your true purpose, these books are designed to instigate infectious positive change that starts with you. Make your mark!

To find out more, visit **www.bkconnection.com**.

Berrett–Koehler
Publishers

Connecting people and ideas
to create a world that works for all

Dear Reader,

Thank you for picking up this book and joining our worldwide community of Berrett-Koehler readers. We share ideas that bring positive change into people's lives, organizations, and society.

To welcome you, we'd like to offer you a free e-book. You can pick from among twelve of our bestselling books by entering the promotional code **BKP92E** here: http://www.bkconnection.com/welcome.

When you claim your free e-book, we'll also send you a copy of our e-newsletter, the *BK Communiqué*. Although you're free to unsubscribe, there are many benefits to sticking around. In every issue of our newsletter you'll find

- A free e-book
- Tips from famous authors
- Discounts on spotlight titles
- Hilarious insider publishing news
- A chance to win a prize for answering a riddle

Best of all, our readers tell us, "Your newsletter is the only one I actually read." So claim your gift today, and please stay in touch!

Sincerely,

Charlotte Ashlock
Steward of the BK Website

Questions? Comments? Contact me at bkcommunity@bkpub.com.

Certified
Corporation
bcorporation.net